The Ri

Gordon Schulz

The Rise of the Mythopoetic Men's Movement

A Psychosocial Analysis

LAP LAMBERT Academic Publishing

Impressum/Imprint (nur für Deutschland/only for Germany)
Bibliografische Information der Deutschen Nationalbibliothek: Die Deutsche Nationalbibliothek verzeichnet diese Publikation in der Deutschen Nationalbibliografie; detaillierte bibliografische Daten sind im Internet über http://dnb.d-nb.de abrufbar.
Alle in diesem Buch genannten Marken und Produktnamen unterliegen warenzeichen-, marken- oder patentrechtlichem Schutz bzw. sind Warenzeichen oder eingetragene Warenzeichen der jeweiligen Inhaber. Die Wiedergabe von Marken, Produktnamen, Gebrauchsnamen, Handelsnamen, Warenbezeichnungen u.s.w. in diesem Werk berechtigt auch ohne besondere Kennzeichnung nicht zu der Annahme, dass solche Namen im Sinne der Warenzeichen- und Markenschutzgesetzgebung als frei zu betrachten wären und daher von jedermann benutzt werden dürften.

Coverbild: www.ingimage.com

Verlag: LAP LAMBERT Academic Publishing GmbH & Co. KG
Dudweiler Landstr. 99, 66123 Saarbrücken, Deutschland
Telefon +49 681 3720-310, Telefax +49 681 3720-3109
Email: info@lap-publishing.com

Herstellung in Deutschland:
Schaltungsdienst Lange o.H.G., Berlin
Books on Demand GmbH, Norderstedt
Reha GmbH, Saarbrücken
Amazon Distribution GmbH, Leipzig
ISBN: 978-3-8465-2480-0

Imprint (only for USA, GB)
Bibliographic information published by the Deutsche Nationalbibliothek: The Deutsche Nationalbibliothek lists this publication in the Deutsche Nationalbibliografie; detailed bibliographic data are available in the Internet at http://dnb.d-nb.de.
Any brand names and product names mentioned in this book are subject to trademark, brand or patent protection and are trademarks or registered trademarks of their respective holders. The use of brand names, product names, common names, trade names, product descriptions etc. even without a particular marking in this works is in no way to be construed to mean that such names may be regarded as unrestricted in respect of trademark and brand protection legislation and could thus be used by anyone.

Cover image: www.ingimage.com

Publisher: LAP LAMBERT Academic Publishing GmbH & Co. KG
Dudweiler Landstr. 99, 66123 Saarbrücken, Germany
Phone +49 681 3720-310, Fax +49 681 3720-3109
Email: info@lap-publishing.com

Printed in the U.S.A.
Printed in the U.K. by (see last page)
ISBN: 978-3-8465-2480-0

Copyright © 2011 by the author and LAP LAMBERT Academic Publishing GmbH & Co. KG and licensors
All rights reserved. Saarbrücken 2011

For my mother, Lucie, and in memory of my father, Gordon, Sr.

Acknowledgements

This book is a revision of a study of the mythopoetic men's movement that I conducted in the mid-1990s. I would like to thank the 10 participants in the Chicago branch of the New Warriors (since renamed the ManKind Project) who allowed me to interview them for this study and who candidly and poignantly shared their personal thoughts, feelings, and experiences with me.

I would also like to thank Dr. Edward Read, the Research Coordinator of ManKind Project International, for facilitating the publication of my manuscript and for giving me helpful feedback on an earlier draft of it.

Table of Contents

Chapter 1: Introduction	5
A Psychosocial Analysis	7
Chapter 2: An Overview of the Mythopoetic Men's Movement	14
Aspects of the Movement	14
Responses to the Movement	22
Chapter 3: The Crisis of Male Identity	28
The Male Breadwinner Ethic	29
The Search for Self-fulfillment	33
Women's Increasing Employment	35
The Sexual Revolution	36
The Feminist Movement	38
The Economic Crisis	41
The Overall Effects	42
Chapter 4: The Problems of Father-Son Relationships	46
The Alienation of Fathers from Sons	48
The Consequences of Paternal Underinvolvement	55
Participants' Perspectives on Their Fathers	58
Chapter 5: The Problems of Men's Relationships	67
The Alienation of Men from Each Other	68
Contemporary Male Relationships	72
Participants' Perspectives on Men's Problems	74

Chapter 6: The Therapeutic Response of the Mythopoetic Men's Movement   79
Bly's Book *Iron John*   80
A Form of Mass Psychotherapy   87

Chapter 7: Participants' Perspectives on the Mythopoetic Men's Movement   93
Experiences in the Movement   93
Views on the All-Male Gatherings   100
Evaluations of the Movement   102

Chapter 8: The Mythopoetic Men's Movement and Gender Politics   108
Participants' Perspectives on Gender Ideals and Feminism   108
Feminist Analysis and Assessment   112
The Need for Progressive Change   118

Chapter 9: Summary   125
The Psychosocial Analysis   125
The Interviews of the Participants   128
The Political Conclusions   129

References   133

Chapter 1:
Introduction

On Monday night, January 8, 1990, American viewers tuned into a strange spectacle on public television. An unidentified man in his 60s, with wildish white hair and a colorful vest and tie, was strumming a bouzouki. Staring ahead into space, almost as if in a trance, the man solemnly intoned, "We are leaving our time now. We are leaving our time now. There are places where time moves more slowly than here." The man then honored the four directions—and "the fifth direction, the vertical one, which is in us— today—here." At that point, he put down his bouzouki and started playing a more upbeat drum. As he drummed, he told a story about a king, a queen, and hunters who go into a forest near a castle and do not return. The camera cut away from the storyteller to show an intently listening all-male audience. He then told his audience that a young man went into the forest with his dog—and a hand rose up out of a pond and pulled the dog down!

The image of the storyteller's face froze, and the title of the program appeared on the screen: *A Gathering of Men* with Bill Moyers and Robert Bly (McCarthy & Ewing, 1990). In the next scene, the familiar image of public television journalist Bill Moyers, the host of the program, appeared. Moyers informed viewers that the program would explore "the confusion that many men feel today about their roles in society and their inner lives as well." He explained that gatherings of men like the one in Austin, Texas, featured in the program, were increasingly taking place and were drawing growing numbers of men. Moyers assured his viewers that in his opinion these gatherings did not reflect men's desire to separate from women or to return to an aggressive, dominating, chauvinistic personality. He stated that "men are drawn to these retreats by a sense of loss, a loss of familiar myths and road maps, but also by a sense of hope." Moyers added that such gatherings give men the chance to see and hear the distinguished poet Robert Bly—the enigmatic white-haired man with the drum—whom the viewers soon learned was the founding father of a so-called men's movement.

In the course of the 90-minute program, Robert Bly discussed many provocative ideas and issues related to the problems of contemporary men. He claimed that modern males have felt a sense of loss and grief over the physical and emotional absence of their fathers since the Industrial Revolution drew them out of the home. He stated that boys consequently no longer receive any knowledge of the "male mode of feeling," which they need in order to develop the confidence of being a man. Bly openly talked about his own early estrangement from his alcoholic father, his "conspiracy" with his mother against his father, and his eventual reconciliation with him in midlife. He also criticized the "John Wayne" model, in which boys are socialized to suppress pain and grief. Bly declared, "The primary experience of the American man is the experience of being inadequate"—due to his inability to achieve at work, his lack of male friends, and his inability to express his feelings with his wife. He said that men must learn to grieve their losses and also develop their inner *Warrior*, which is their sense of determination and commitment. Because of the lack of institutionalized male initiation in modern society and the devaluation of fathers in popular culture, the young man must find a male mentor, or a *male mother*, who can nurture, guide, encourage, and admire him. Bly concluded that a woman can bring forth a boy from a fetus, but only a man can bring forth a man from a boy.

Near the end of the program, Bill Moyers spoke briefly with some of the participants at the Austin gathering. He asked one of them if he was confused about what it means to be a man today. The man replied that he had received many "contradictory signals" in his life, including messages to be both Superman and Superwoman. A second man disclosed that he feels safer talking with men than with women. Another explained that men are emotionally dependent on women, despite men's material privileges vis-à-vis women. Still another said that men cannot really talk with each other about their feelings. One man volunteered that he wants to "heal" his relationship with his father. Another man, choking back the emotion, spoke poignantly about being rejected by his now-deceased father. The first man who spoke said that he had come to the weekend retreat to see and hear one of the few strong, clear, and powerful men in the world today—Robert Bly. He explained that there was a "vacuum of powerful male men in the world, male models of clarity, initiated men, that we males are trying to rediscover fire. And that is the quest."

Thus, with the broadcast of this television special, the American public was introduced to the mythopoetic men's movement, or, simply, the men's movement, as it is commonly known. Quietly started by Robert Bly in the early 1980s, the men's movement is a personal-development movement that is devoted to redefining masculinity and exploring the psychology and personal problems of contemporary men. It consists largely of men's mutual support groups, workshops, conferences, and weekend retreats. These gatherings of men, as they are called, feature various activities, including didactic instruction, mythic storytelling, poetry reading, group therapy-like exercises, drumming, dancing, and enactment of rituals. The main professed goals of the men's movement are to rebuild and revitalize male community and to heal the psychological wounds of men, primarily through ritual male bonding.

Following the broadcast of *A Gathering of Men*, the men's movement received much public attention for the next few years. This attention increased with the publication of *Iron John*, Bly's book about male initiation, which became a best-seller in 1991. On television, the men's movement was discussed on such popular talk shows as *Oprah* and *Donahue*. It was also featured—and lampooned—in episodes of situation comedies, including *Cheers* and *Murphy Brown*. Feminists denounced it, claiming that it was part of the conservative backlash against the women's movement. Although the mass media often mocked it, this men's movement clearly raised serious issues that struck a chord with many men. By 1991, an estimated 100,000 men had participated in some kind of men's movement event (Schwalbe, 1996). At the end of 1991, *People* magazine named Robert Bly one of the 25 most intriguing people of the year. Although the media attention decreased significantly by the mid-1990s, the men's movement has continued to draw men to its activities and organizations to date.

A Psychosocial Analysis

Despite its obvious relevance to the related fields of psychology and psychotherapy, few psychologists or social scientists had researched the mythopoetic men's movement at the time that this study was conducted in the mid-1990s. The purpose of this book is to provide a psychosocial analysis of the rise of the men's movement, one that is partly based on case studies of participants. The primary objective is to discuss and explain the psychological, sociological, and historical factors that gave rise to the movement in the United States in the 1980s and early 1990s. A secondary objective is to examine, empathically yet critically, the presenting problems of men in the movement, the grievances that the movement makes on behalf of men, and the solutions that it proposes. The ultimate goal is to illuminate contemporary American male experience and to identify the broader societal and institutional changes that must be made in order to solve the legitimate problems of men as a sex.

The case studies presented in this analysis consist of structured, in-depth interviews of 10 men who had been active in the men's movement in the Chicago area prior to 1994. All of the men had been involved at some point with the Chicago branch of the New Warriors, a men's movement organization. Inspired by Robert Bly, the New Warriors were founded in 1984 in Wisconsin by psychotherapist Bill Kauth, ex-Marine and industrial engineer Rich Tosi, and personal-growth expert Ron Hering (Kauth, 1992a; Kuznik, 1994). The professed main goal of the New Warriors was to provide men with male initiation—"an accelerated learning experience that helps men gain purpose, define their mission, and face the obstacles that keep them from the fulfillment of that mission" (Kauth, 1992a, pp. 128-129). While the New Warriors rejected the old dominating and acquisitive warrior as obsolete, they championed the "Warrior of the Heart"—a man with integrity and direction—a man who is "wild and gentle, tough and loving, fierce and perceptive" (p. 129). The New Warriors later renamed themselves the ManKind Project due to the "negative baggage" associated with the word "warrior" (Barton, 2000, p. xii).

All of the men interviewed in this study had participated in the two main activities that the New Warriors offered: the New Warrior Training Adventure weekend retreat and the follow-up Integration Group, a weekly support group. The length of time that the men participated in their respective Integration Groups ranged from 3 months to 5 years, with an average of 17 months. Seven men were recruited by randomly calling names on a phone list of men who had completed the weekend retreat (a phone list which the author received upon completing the retreat himself). Two men were recruited by advertising in the newsletter of the Chicago New Warriors. One was recruited by advertising in a flier distributed at the Third Chicago Men's Conference. In the interviews, which were conducted in 1994, the men were asked to discuss their life experiences, their involvement in the men's movement, and their views on various gender issues. Selective material from these interviews will be presented in chapters 4, 5, 7, and 8.

Demographic information about the men interviewed included the following findings. All 10 men were Caucasian, mostly of Northern European descent. The ages of the men ranged from 32 to 61, with an average age of 42. Regarding religion, four described themselves as Roman Catholic, three as Protestant, one as Buddhist, one as interested in Buddhism, and one as agnostic. Regarding sexual orientation, eight identified as heterosexual, one as gay, and one as bisexual. Three of the men were married, three divorced, two separated, and two never married. Six were fathers. Most of the men were professionals, managers, or businessmen. Annual individual income ranged from $20,000 to $700,000, with a median income of $52,000. Overall, the demographic profile of this sample is very similar to the demographic profile of the 200 men that Osherson (1992) surveyed at men's movement workshops, in terms of age, marital status, fatherhood status, occupation, and income. The most significant difference is the percentage of men who identified as gay or bisexual—only 5% in Osherson's study, compared to a full 20% in this study. It is not clear whether the greater percentage of men who identified as gay or bisexual in this study was representative of the New Warriors or was due to chance, given the small sample size, or to some other, unknown factor.

In addition to drawing on these interviews, the analysis draws on the author's own limited personal involvement as both an observer and participant. This involvement included attending three weekend conferences in Chicago: "A Day for Men: The Energies of the Warrior," led by Robert Moore and Douglas Gillette, in November 1991; "Man in the Maze: The Second Chicago Men's Conference," in February 1993; and "Sharpening the Focus: The Third Chicago Men's Conference," in February 1994. I also participated in the New Warrior Training Adventure weekend retreat in March 1994. After the retreat, I joined one of the Integration Groups for the preliminary 2-month period.

Of all these activities, the most useful one for the purposes of this study was the weekend retreat. More than the others, the retreat helped me to understand the powerful appeal that the men's movement has for the men who have become active in it or whose lives it has touched. Although my experiences at the retreat very much informed my understanding of the movement, I will not discuss the events of that weekend or any of the specific activities, techniques, and rituals that were conducted there. The reason for my nondisclosure is that I, along with all others who participated in the retreat, agreed in writing not to write about the weekend, as a requirement for admission. The rationale that the New Warriors gave for this requirement is that it protects the confidentiality of the participants' experiences and the supposed sacredness of the rituals. Considering the often hostile coverage of the men's movement by the mass media, the policy was probably aimed also at preventing negative publicity that might deter prospective participants from enrolling in the retreat. Additionally, advance knowledge of the retreat's events and activities might have diminished their impact and effectiveness. In any case, my observance of the written agreement not to divulge does not unduly limit my analysis, as the key to understanding the men's movement does not lie in knowing the specific activities of the New Warrior Training Adventure weekend retreat. Rather, it lies in knowing the issues, problems, and life experiences of the men, the movement's general response to them, and the specific activities that are common to movement organizations across the country and that have been identified as such by other writers. All of these elements will be discussed here.

While the analysis draws on the case studies and the author's own personal involvement, it is mainly based on theory and findings from the psychological, sociological, and historical literature on and relevant to American men. The focus is on white middle-class middle-aged heterosexual men because they are the main constituents of the men's movement. A central underlying assumption of the analysis is that the meaning of masculinity is largely socially constructed, not biologically determined, and that it varies across cultures, through history, between different groups within a given culture (e.g., social class and race), and across the life span. Such a view is clearly at odds with the psychobiological essentialism of Jungian psychology, which is a dominant feature of the ideology of the men's movement. Against the Jungian notion of a "deep" or "mature" or "true" masculinity based on natural and unchanging sex-linked *archetypes*, this analysis draws on social constructionist theories of gender identity.

One of theses theories is Bem's (1993) gender schema theory. According to Bem, people internalize the hidden assumptions about gender embedded in their culture, predisposing them to construct identities that are consistent with those assumptions.

Individual males and females are motivated to construct conventional, polarized masculine or feminine personalities, respectively, in gender-polarizing societies. Such societies superimpose male-female difference on virtually every aspect of human experience, including modes of dress, social roles, and ways of expressing emotion and experiencing sexual desire. In gender-polarizing societies, people reject any ways of behaving that are not considered appropriate for their respective gender, so that they can satisfy the needs of their conventionally masculine or feminine identities. Also, people are motivated to fulfill gender role expectations to gain social approval and to adapt to situations (Pleck, 1981).

Another social constructionist theory on which this analysis draws is Hantover's (1981) theory of masculine anxiety. Hantover identified two types of masculine anxiety, both of which flow from gender role strain. The first type of anxiety occurs when the male is unclear about his gender role expectations or when his gender role expectations conflict with each other. For example, a male may feel anxiety in response to conflicting expectations to be dominant and to be a good mixer and one of the boys. The second type of anxiety occurs in conditions in which the male lacks opportunities to act on and fulfill his gender role expectations. For example, a man working in a white-collar job in a modern bureaucracy or in the service sector of the economy may feel anxiety because he does not enjoy the opportunity to fulfill the traditional gender role expectations to be autonomous, active, and masterful. Hantover explained that men can reduce masculine anxiety either by retaining the gender role tradition and creating new ways to affirm it or by redefining masculinity altogether. Additionally, men have historically reduced the anxiety associated with gender role strain by conforming to other aspects of the male role in an exaggerated, compensatory way (Pleck, 1981) and by emphasizing and increasing the differences between the cultural definitions of masculinity and femininity (Stearns, 1990).

A third theory on which this analysis draws is Weinstein and Platt's (1973) psychoanalytic sociological theory of collective behavior. Weinstein and Platt observed that people generally internalize the prevailing standards and expectations of their culture regarding morality, achievement and mastery, and the satisfaction of basic needs. People tend to act according to their internalized values to the extent that they are able to do so and to the extent that others do so. However, if people are unable to do so or if others do not do so, their identities will be threatened, damaging self-esteem and generating anxiety. People may collectively rebel or challenge existing authority and values when certain social structural changes (e.g., industrialization, urbanization, economic crisis, war, etc.) cause them to violate internalized values. People tend to experience such a violation as a loss. Consequently, they will potentially turn to charismatic leaders to help them cope with the loss and help them solve their problems.

    The central thesis of this book is that the mythopoetic men's movement arose in the 1980s and early 1990s primarily in response to a crisis of male identity that men, especially middle-class men, have widely experienced in varying degrees in the United States since the 1970s. This crisis of male identity consists mainly of the collective experience of loss produced by challenges to traditional masculinity, particularly its central feature, the male breadwinner ethic. This crisis of male identity has enabled and motivated men to reflect critically upon and reevaluate certain problems of traditional male experience, including fathers' relative underinvolvement in child rearing and men's relative lack of emotional intimacy in interpersonal relationships, especially with each other. Drawing on the existing therapeutic culture, Robert Bly and other charismatic leaders of the men's movement responded to the contemporary crisis of male identity and the problems of traditional male experience by offering to heal these socially inflicted psychological wounds. The experience of male bonding in the all-male gatherings of the movement also helped men heal their wounds and meet their more basic needs for general support, male validation, and personal growth and development.

    This analysis is mainly concerned with the identity, experience, and legitimate problems of men as a sex. However, it does take feminist concerns into serious consideration. Indeed, problems of men are characterized here as legitimate partly to the extent that they can be solved without infringing on the rights of women. Although some men's movement supporters might object to defining men's problems in terms of their meaning for women, it is necessary to do so, at least partly, because men can potentially experience or identify any feminist challenge to male privilege and sexism as a "problem." Unlike some men's movement supporters who are indifferent or even hostile to feminism in their advocacy of a new model of masculinity, I argue that any model of masculinity must be at least compatible with, if not explicitly supportive of, gender equality to be worthy of support itself. However, unlike most feminist critics who demand that the men's movement adopt an explicitly feminist orientation in order to receive support, I hold the movement to the considerably less stringent standard that it merely not add to the oppression of women.

My position on this issue is not intended to minimize the pressing need for a strong feminist movement to fight for women's liberation. On the contrary, I will argue that part of the solution to men's legitimate problems, as well as to women's oppression, ultimately lies with the implementation of a feminist political agenda. However, I also view men's therapeutic efforts to heal their psychological wounds as valid in and of themselves. Moreover, I do not think that this particular men's movement can maintain itself if it adopts a substantive feminist orientation in practice, given that the movement is a primarily personal-development movement that is focused on the psychological needs of men. While I share some of the concerns of feminist critics, I believe that on the whole the men's movement in its present form does not constitute a threat to the struggle for gender equality. Thus, this analysis is generally less critical of and more sympathetic to the men's movement than most feminist analyses have been.

Chapter 2:
An Overview of the Mythopoetic Men's Movement

This chapter consists of a literature review of the mythopoetic men's movement through the mid-1990s, when the current study was conducted. Movement insiders, journalists, and feminist critics wrote most of the literature on the men's movement, mostly in the early1990s. As previously mentioned, social scientists and other scholars conducted little research on the subject. The first part of this overview is a presentation of the main aspects of the movement, including its history, ideology, structure, processes, and constituency. The second part is a presentation of the responses to the men's movement, including both sympathetic and hostile responses by outside observers and commentators. The chapter concludes with a brief summary critique of this literature.

Aspects of the Movement

Although it is usually referred to as *the* men's movement, the mythopoetic men's movement is only one of several men's movements that have appeared in the United States since the early 1970s. While these different movements share some concerns and historical precipitants, they are nonetheless distinct currents with largely different focuses, goals, ideologies, organizations, and constituencies (Harding, 1992a). The profeminist men's movement is a political current that opposes sexism and homophobia and seeks to mobilize men in support of the agendas of the feminist and gay movements. The men's rights/fathers' rights movement, also a political current, lobbies for legislative changes in child custody, child support awards, the rights of unmarried fathers, and abortion, to benefit men. The male recovery movement, a therapeutic current which evolved out of 12-step programs like Alcoholics Anonymous, focuses on men's recovery from addiction, with an emphasis on the connection between addiction and traditional masculinity. In the mid-1990s, a religious men's movement emerged—the Promise Keepers—that drew men to all-male gatherings in sports arenas for prayer, repentance, male bonding, and commitment to conservative Christian values (Stoltenberg, 1995).

The mythopoetic men's movement is probably the best-known of the men's movements. However, the designation *mythopoetic* was not widely used either inside or outside the movement. One of the veteran leaders of the movement, Shepherd Bliss, chose the word *mythopoetic*, a literary term that means creating or making myth, to describe the movement in an article in the *Yoga Journal* in 1986 (Bliss, 1986). Robert Bly reportedly preferred *a movement among men* (Becker, 1992), or simply *men's work* (Shewey, 1992), over *men's movement*, which misleadingly implies a unified body with a central structure. One writer in the movement asserted that there really was not a men's movement, which suggests political action, but rather "something powerful moving *in* and *between* men, an emotional and spiritual surge of loving and powerful male energy" (Farmer, 1991, p. xiv). Responding to commentators who disputed the very existence of the movement because of the political connotations of the term, Harding (1992a) explained the difference between the men's movement and a political movement, such as the women's movement:

> Unlike the women's movement, which is largely outwardly directed, aimed at changing laws, societal structures, and other people's way of thinking, the men's movement is inwardly directed. It is generally much less concerned with new dogmas and presuming to "correct" other people's thought patterns and behavior than it is with encouraging men to find and follow their individual path, that personal myth or mission that will give meaning and form to their lives (p. xii).

Thus, the mythopoetic men's movement is primarily a personal-development movement. (For the sake of brevity, I will frequently refer to the subject of this book as *the men's movement*, as it is commonly known, despite the imprecision of this designation.) Becker (1992) identified five key themes of the men's movement. One, the movement claimed that males need to be initiated from boyhood into manhood. It held that boys must make a decisive, qualitative break from their mothers, then bond with their fathers, and finally separate from their fathers as well, in order to become their own men. Two, the movement encouraged men to engage in "soul-tending" (p. 90). Such soul-tending meant that men introspect, examine their feelings, grieve their emotional wounds, and learn from them. Three, the movement challenged men to find strength and support in the company of other men. They must seek out male peers as well as male mentors, counselors, and role models to help them learn how to become men. Four, the movement drew on various symbolic material—including myths, fairy tales, rituals, and poems—to glean universal human truths and to facilitate healing. Five, the movement encouraged men to access and develop such qualities as initiative, forthrightness, resolve, and respect for the earth.

As previously mentioned, the distinguished poet Robert Bly started the men's movement (Johnston, 1992; Morrow, 1991; Wagenheim, 1990). The son of a Minnesota farmer and a graduate of Harvard, Bly first received national recognition in 1968, when he won the National Book Award for poetry, for his collection *The Light Around the Body*. In the 1970s, he gave feminist spiritualist seminars on the subject of the Great Mother in fairy tales and myths. In the course of this work, he discovered that there were few fairy tales about a boy's growth into a man. This discovery, coupled with the beginnings of an eventual reconciliation with his alcoholic father, spurred his interest in men's issues. It also inspired him to research the Grimm Brothers' fairy tale "Iron Hans," about a prince who is initiated into manhood by a Wild Man that he discovers at the bottom of a pond—a story that greatly influenced Bly's ideas about male initiation.

In 1981, Bly was invited to lead a workshop for about 40 men at the Lama commune in New Mexico, a stint that launched a career in giving presentations to men about men, masculinity, and male initiation. In his presentations, Bly assumed the dual role of healer and spiritual guide, a role that he may have borrowed from the influential New Age movement (Lewis, 1992). One observer of his presentations described him as "a stand-up comic, troubadour, storyteller, literary critic, group therapist, and emotional catalyst all in one" (Johnston, 1992, p. 31). Another commentator described his personal style as "one part mad professor, one part guidance counselor, one part wide-eyed school boy" (Wagenheim, 1990, p. 40). In 1982, an interview with Bly, entitled "What Men Really Want," was published in *New Age* magazine (Bly, 1982), the event that has been cited as marking the rise of the men's movement (Clatterbaugh, 1990). In 1990, the movement became more visible and grew following the broadcast of Bill Moyers' PBS special, *A Gathering of Men*. Later that year, the movement was further bolstered by the publication of *Iron John*, Bly's book about the "Iron Hans" fairy tale, which remained on the *New York Times* hardcover best-seller list for 62 weeks.

In *Iron John*, which was widely regarded as the bible of the men's movement, Bly (1990) expounded his beliefs about men, masculinity, and male initiation. Bly criticized what he called the *Fifties male*, the model of manhood that dominated the United States in the 1950s and that is characterized by aggressiveness, emotional inexpressiveness, a commitment to breadwinning, and a lack of sensitivity and compassion. Bly also criticized what he called the *Sixties-Seventies man*, or *soft male*, a model of manhood that is characterized by a feminine-identified gentleness and sensitivity and a lack of energy, resolve, and assertiveness. As an alternative to both of these faulty models of manhood, Bly proposed a third model—the model of *deep masculinity*, or the *Wild Man*—which is characterized by spontaneity, decisiveness, sensualness, and an affinity with nature. Bly attributed the underdevelopment of this supposedly innate deep masculinity in modern males to the diminution of the father-son bond with the advent of the Industrial Revolution. Bly explained that the Industrial Revolution separated fathers and sons, who previously had worked together on the land or in a trade in preindustrial society, by drawing fathers out of their homes and into city offices and factories, leaving their sons to be raised primarily by their mothers. Bly argued that contemporary males must access and develop their deep masculinity by breaking from their mothers and by being initiated into the community of men. To contribute to this process, Bly offered his interpretation of, and the insights that he gleaned from, the "Iron Hans" fairy tale.

Another important book of the men's movement was *King, Warrior, Magician, Lover: Rediscovering the Mature Masculine*, co-authored by Robert Moore and Douglas Gillette (1990), a Jungian psychoanalyst and a Jungian counselor, respectively. Like Bly, Moore and Gillette identified a serious crisis of masculine identity in Western society. They attributed this crisis to three main factors: (1) the breakdown of the traditional family and the concomitant disappearance, either physical or emotional, of fathers in their children's lives; (2) the disappearance of ritual processes for initiating boys into manhood in the wake of the Protestant Reformation and the Enlightenment; and (3) patriarchy, the social and cultural organization of male dominance, which, they claimed, is based on immature masculinity, i.e., the boy's fear of women and men. Moore and Gillette posited that the combination of these three factors prevents males from accessing and developing the archetypes of mature masculinity, which, in Jungian psychology, are genetically inherited instinctual blueprints that pattern the thoughts, feelings, and behaviors of men. The four main archetypes of manhood are the King, providing order and guidance; the Warrior, providing force when needed; the Magician, providing knowledge and mastery;

and the Lover, providing play, sensuality, and love. When these four archetypes are not accessed and properly developed, the individual man will express distortions of their qualities in a form of immature masculinity, e.g., tyranny, ineffectualness, sadism, masochism, manipulation, addiction, and impotence. Moore and Gillett concluded that contemporary men must reinstitute the ritual practice of male initiation in order to transcend immature masculinity and its destructive consequences.

    Other writers in the men's movement focused on other issues that are central to the male experience. For example, Marvin Allen (1993), the director of the Texas Men's Institute and the founder of the Texas Wildmen Gatherings, identified three main sources of men's problems: (1) gender conditioning, in which males are socialized to suppress their emotions; (2) dysfunctional parents, such as critical, passive, abusive, or neglectful fathers and smothering, seductive, critical, or abusive mothers; and (3) inadequate social skills. The consequences of these three factors is that men struggle with intimacy, work, some form of addiction or compulsive behavior, and difficulty controlling or expressing anger. Men's movement spokesmen agreed that the paramount problem of males was the childhood experience of paternal absence and underinvolvement, which was described in terms of a wound—*the father wound*. Farmer (1991) elaborated:

> Most of us men bear deep wounds from our relationships with our fathers. We did not experience having them available and accessible as we were growing up. Whether they were disciplinarians or passive, uninvolved bystanders, what we each got was a piece of our fathers. Although we experience other wounds from the male parent, the most damaging wound we experience as boys, the one that continues to have its effects on us as men, is the wound caused by his absence or remoteness (p. 24).

    To address the father wound and other problems of men, the men's movement organized gatherings of men. Although what occurred at these gatherings varied greatly from place to place, in some parts of the country they included support groups, councils, and retreats that occur at regular, specified times (Harding, 1992b). The support group met on a weekly or biweekly basis, usually was comprised of between five and ten men, and was the foundation of the movement. The purpose of the support group was for men to work on themselves with the help of a regular group of others committed to self-exploration. The council met on a monthly basis, attracted between 50 and 300 men, and offered a less intimate and more formal and structured format. The purpose of the council meeting was to take care of organizational business, provide a special presentation, discuss a particular issue or topic, and sell movement literature and audio-tapes. The retreat occurred once or twice a year, typically in the fall and spring, comprised 20 to 150 men, and was set in summer campsites in the country. The purpose of the retreat was to provide men with a respite from their everyday lives and to give them an extraordinary opportunity for intense personal healing and growth.

    Bliss (1992) described the events that typically unfolded at the mythopoetic men's retreats that he led. Bliss made the qualification that the philosophy and formats of men's retreats varied greatly, depending largely on the perspective of the given leadership, or presenting staff. The professed purpose of Bliss' retreats was to facilitate recovery, discovery, restoration of the male community, and development of deep masculinity, which is characterized by vitality, spontaneity, boldness, vigor, sensitivity, and gentility. Common titles of his retreats, intended to imply a spiritual quest or movement, included "Rediscovering the Deep Masculine" and "Journey into the Male Wilderness." The retreats were restricted to men in order to provide a "safe—but not tame environment" for men to fully express their feelings without the potentially inhibiting presence of women (p. 97). The three main activities were storytelling, poetry, and drumming, which were supplemented with didactic instruction, guided meditation and fantasy, mask-making, dance, plays, and a concluding celebration. Personal disclosures that focused on relationships with other men, especially fathers and brothers, tended to produce the greatest emotional expressions of love and anger. Bliss observed that during the retreats, "many extremes are touched—from sadness to ecstasy, remembering experiences from long ago—and ongoing friendships are often deepened or initiated" (p. 99).

    An integral element of the weekend retreats, for which they received much attention, was the use of rituals, many of which were borrowed from Native American culture. Kauth (1992b) explained that the purpose of the rituals in men's groups was "to bring us together with shared intention and focus, to mutually create the safety necessary for change to happen, to enact a certain mythology and sometimes to create an altered state of consciousness" (p. 203). One important ritual of the men's gatherings was drumming, which was used to create a "sacred space" in which to do psychological and spiritual work. Another key ritual was the use of the *talking stick*, which was a staff, often carved or decorated with feathers and fur, that gave the bearer the right to be heard without interruption. The *sweat lodge* was an enclosed space in which men gather, nude or semi-nude, to be physically and spiritually purified by the rising temperature produced by heating rocks. In the *spirit chair* rite, the participants supposedly summoned the spirit of a Warrior—a deceased man, whom the participants admired—who then sat with them in the gatherings for the purpose of inspiring them. *Smudging* involved the smudging of burned sage and cedar sticks onto the bodies of the participants to symbolize the washing away of negative energies. A less formal or more spontaneous ritual of men's gatherings was the act of touching, especially hugging, which directly challenged the traditional American taboo against physical affection between men.

Many outside observers, especially the mass media, focused on the rituals and other aspects of the men's movement that appeared exotic, bizarre, whimsical, pretentious, or even comical in mainstream American culture. Photographs taken at weekend retreats that appeared in both popular magazines and movement publications showed men doing a variety of unusual things, including wearing nothing but loincloths, wearing body paint, wearing animal masks, holding spears, dancing with each other, hugging each other, hugging trees, sitting in trees, skinny-dipping, drumming, weeping, etc. While critics of these aspects mocked them or called them vulgar, contrived, or silly, defenders claimed that within the context of the retreat they were sacred, growth-producing, and empowering (Harding, 1992c). Bly chastised the media for its distorted, sensationalistic coverage of the men's movement and for diverting public attention away from the core, substantive issues with which the movement was concerned. Overstating his point somewhat, Bly declared, "The men's movement really has nothing to do with going out in the woods, as the media like to say, and dancing around naked" (pp. 30-31). Osherson (1992) explained that the main activity of men's gatherings was not enactment of rituals but discussion of basic life issues of men, e.g., being a good father, resolving conflicts with one's own father, feeling like a real man at home, and saving one's marriage.

While the personal problems and issues with which men dealt in men's movement forums were diverse, the constituency of the movement was fairly homogenous demographically. Most of the men active in the movement were white, middle class, middle-aged, and heterosexual. The regional strongholds of the movement were the Midwest, Colorado, and greater Washington, D.C. (Harding, 1992a). In their survey of attendants of a variety of retreats and conferences in different parts of the country, Kimmel and Kaufman (1994) found that 98 to 100% of the men were white; that professional, white-collar, and managerial men outnumbered blue-collar and other working-class men; that most of the men were between the ages of 40 and 55; and that the number of gay men never exceeded 5%. In his survey of 200 participants from men's movement events around the country, using both questionnaires and in-depth interviews, Osherson (1992) found that the typical participant was a professional, 43 years old, married, never divorced, with children at home. Osherson also found that one-third were under 40 years old and one-third over 50 years old; that 48% had annual incomes between $20,000 and $50,000 and 41% between $50,000 and $100,000; that 95% were heterosexual and 5% gay or bisexual; that two-thirds of the men were fathers; and that one-third of them identified themselves as the victim and/or perpetrator of physical or sexual abuse.

Perhaps the single demographic variable that received the most attention in discussions of the men's movement was age—the striking fact that most participants were middle-aged. While the aforementioned surveys found that most of the men were over 40, leaders of the movement similarly estimated the average age of the men who attended retreats to be about 40 years old (Bliss, 1992; Meade, 1993), with most tending to be between 35 and 55 years old (Harding, 1992a). Meade (1993) claimed that men at midlife were especially inclined to join the movement and explore the meaning of manhood because "they inherit the crises of the elders that preceded them and they are being pushed by the generation that follows" (p. 14). More importantly, Meade asserted, "the 'midlife crisis' represents another period of initiation, when all the smoldering issues of previous life stages as well as those of the present are ignited" (p. 14). He explained that men at midlife must face and come to terms with past losses, such as divorce, early failures, deaths, accidents, lost loves, and suppressed desires. Consequently, such men were more emotionally open to introspection, one of the central activities of the men's movement.

Responses to the Movement

Responses to the mythopoetic men's movement by commentators ranged from sympathy, through ridicule, to serious hostility. Among those sympathetic commentators were men who either participated in weekend retreats or spoke to men who had done so. Gabriel (1990) participated in a retreat called the Wildman Gathering, in North Texas, and he reported that the men at the retreat expressed much grief about the poor quality of their relationships with their fathers and much confusion about living up to conventional expectations of masculinity. Gabriel observed that most men seem to want "more forums in which they can talk directly to one another, a kind of recovery program for victims of errant notions of masculinity, a sort of Men's Anonymous" (p. 47). In a cover story for *Newsweek* magazine, Adler (1991) spoke to participants who reportedly found the retreats to be profoundly moving, as the retreats provided them with opportunities to talk about their feelings and grieve their losses, such as the breakup of a marriage or the death of a father. Adler thus described the men's movement in the following poetic terms: "Fed up with leading lives of quiet desperation, men are pouring their hearts out to one another, seeking comfort in the power of brotherhood" (p. 46).

Two sympathetic commentators who attended weekend conferences and retreats led by Robert Bly shared their observations. Shewey (1992) claimed that these gatherings enabled men to do "soul work" (p. 36). He suggested that such soul work helped isolated men find social support, psychologically wounded men healing, and emotionally numb men access to and expression of their feelings. Gilbert (1992) reported that the men participating in a retreat spoke about neglect, abandonment, physical/sexual/emotional abuse, addiction, anger, emptiness, and confusion. Similar to Gabriel, Gilbert concluded that "what men seemed to value and want the most, more than percussion and ritual, was an opportunity to talk openly about their experiences and struggles as men" (p. 65).

Another group of commentators, who called themselves profeminist men, identified positive aspects of the movement as part of a mixed overall assessment. Kimmel (1993) claimed that the movement "does valuable work in breaking down men's isolation from one another, and giving permission for men to experience deep feelings" (p. i). Dash (1993) identified three positive contributions of the movement: (1) the recognition of the bankruptcy of contemporary masculinity, which is based on material acquisition and the domination of women; (2) the recognition that the solution to this problem lies in the collective work or community of men, not in individual effort alone or in women; and (3) the recognition that the solution also lies in inner psychological work. Kupers (1993) identified three other elements as positive: (1) Bly's instruction to men to forgive their fathers for their inadequacies and misdeeds, (2) Bly's recognition of the boy's need to individuate from his mother, and (3) Bly's validation of certain specifically male styles of interacting and relating to one another. Lastly, Schwalbe (1993, 1996) acknowledged the therapeutic nature of the movement gatherings, especially for those men with serious psychological wounds.

Most other commentators were singularly hostile. Morrow (1991) interpreted the men's movement as the transformation of Bly's personal struggle with his alcoholic father into a phenomenon of celebrity and mass therapy that has the "quality of Americans' making fools of themselves in brave pop quests for salvation" (p. 54). Stanton (1991) called the movement "a therapeutic circus of monied fellows" who "growl and yodel to protect what's theirs (their balls, among other things), weep and moan about what they've lost (their minds, it seems), and kick the world's ass without apology while smiling at feminists" (p. 113). Addressing the relationship between a charismatic leader and his followers, Carol Bly (1992), Robert Bly's ex-wife, described the movement as based on "an unconscious deal between a big-time warrior wannabe and a wimpy warrior wannabe" (p. 6). Rosen (1992) interpreted the movement as an attempt by self-indulgent white middle-class men to join the "victim culture" (p. 539). Alexie (1992) criticized the movement for appropriating Native American rituals as solutions to the problems of white men while neglecting to provide solutions to the problems of Native Americans. Gordon (1991) simply dismissed the movement as "a bunch of men not having enough to do with their time" (p. 13).

The most serious criticisms came from feminists, scholars as well as activists. The following remarks of four prominent feminists were representative of the general attitudes, concerns, and sentiments of the majority of feminists who wrote about the men's movement. Betty Friedan, author of *The Feminine Mystique* and cofounder of the National Organization for Women, commented, "These Wildman and Warrior gatherings are an attempt to rigidify the machismo mask that actually may or may not have aided the original caveman in his survival" (Stanton, 1991, p. 118). Gloria Steinem (1992), cofounder of *Ms.* magazine, queried, "Is the men's movement uprooting the politics of patriarchy, or just giving them a new face?" (p. vii). Robin Morgan, editor of *Sisterhood is Powerful* and editor-in-chief of *Ms.* magazine, declared, "This movement is at best irrelevant, even hilarious, and at worst an unsettling new form of male bonding" (Harding, 1992d, p. 230). Susan Faludi, author of *Backlash: The Undeclared War Against American Women* (1991), claimed, "The true subject of Bly's weekends, after all, is not love and sex, but power—how to wrest it from women and how to mobilize it for men" (p. 310).

Feminist writers made several specific criticisms of the men's movement. One aspect of the movement that they repeatedly criticized is its biological essentialism, its postulation of basic, innate and fixed psychological differences between males and females across time and place (Brown, 1992; Clatterbaugh, 1993; Connell, 1992; Kimmel & Kaufman, 1994; Samuels, 1992). Another problem that feminists identified is the movement's exclusion of women from gatherings, its support for sons breaking from mothers, and its rejection of a feminine identification in males (Caputi & MacKenzie, 1992; Connell, 1992; Doubiago, 1992; Eisler, 1992; Johnston, 1992; Kupers, 1993). Feminists also criticized the movement for involving the imagery of warriors and utilizing fairy tales, which contain patriarchal values (Caputi & MacKenzie, 1992; Clatterbaugh, 1993; Connell, 1992; Steinem, 1992). Perhaps the biggest criticism that feminists made of the movement was that by focusing on men's personal problems and individual change, it diverted attention away from men's responsibility for women's oppression and obscured the need for social change to eradicate that oppression (Clatterbaugh, 1993; Connell, 1992; Hooks, 1992; Kupers, 1993; Samuels, 1992). Furthermore, feminists generally held that the men's movement represented part of the conservative backlash against the women's movement (Beneke, 1993; Connell, 1992; Faludi, 1991; Johnston, 1992). Indeed, feminists interpreted participants in the men's movement as aiming to restore traditional norms of masculinity and femininity and to reassert male dominance (Kimmel & Kaufman, 1994).

Defenders of the men's movement generally did not address these specific criticisms directly in writing (Kimmel, 1996), but they responded to the general charge that the men's movement was antifeminist. Bly (1990) assured his readers that his book *Iron John* "does not seek to turn men against women, nor to return men to the domineering mode that has led to repression of women and their values for centuries" (p. x). He insisted that the men's movement is not an antifeminist backlash and that men working with men does not imply a rejection of women (Wagenheim, 1990). Adler (1991) observed that nowhere does Bly imply that men should dominate women, and he pointed out that the movement does not have a political or social agenda. Lee (1991), the publisher of *MAN!* magazine, addressed women's understandable skepticism and suspicion toward the men's movement: "Is it just another way for men to form one more elitist and exclusive club that will be oppressive to women and children? The answer is a very firm NO" (p. 91). Harding (1992a) asserted that "the mythopoetic majority are apples that exist peaceably enough with women's-issue oranges but have their focus principally on other matters" (p. xvi). One (unusual) feminist commentator stated that she perceived in the men's movement not a celebration of male domination, "but simply a plea for a world where there are people in general and men in particular to whom one can *look up*" (Ellis, 1994, p. 14).

Other defenders of the men's movement were stronger in their responses to feminists. Kipnis (1991) reported that it is rare that denigrating sentiments about women are expressed at men's gatherings, but he claimed that men resent the powerful antimale trends in popular culture. Moore and Gillette (1990) acknowledged that patriarchy is a problem, but they opposed what they perceived as "an outright demonization of men and a slander against masculinity" perpetrated by some feminists (p. 156). One anonymous local leader of the men's movement declared, "I'm tired of all the male-bashing. I just can't listen to women's issues anymore while passively watching so many men go down the tubes" (Kipnis & Hingston, 1993, p. 69). Harding (1992a) observed, "Wholesale male bashing is a politically correct activity practiced freely by those who wouldn't dream of making similar sweeping criticisms about Jews, blacks, or women" (p. xi).

While most feminist commentators criticized the men's movement as antifeminist, other feminist analysts characterized it as *masculinist* (Basow, 1992; Kimmel, 1995; Kimmel & Kaufman, 1994; Rotundo, 1993). Whereas antifeminists oppose women's entry into the public sphere and their struggle for equality with men in that sphere, masculinists are concerned with women's control over childhood socialization, especially of boys, and the consequent feminization of males. Thus, the contemporary men's movement, with its emphasis on men separating from women and boys separating from mothers, was similar to a masculinist movement that arose among urban middle-class men in the United States in the late 1800s. In response to the modern industrial removal of the father from the home, males in Victorian America sought to bolster their besieged gender identities through male bonding in fraternal lodges and college fraternities. Like the participants in the contemporary men's movement who take to the wilderness, enact Native American rituals, and imitate animals, these late 19th-century men invoked the image of a "primitive masculinity," appropriated the rites of African natives, and likened themselves to wild animals. Kimmel and Kaufman (1994) characterized both these masculinist movements, in terms of individual psychological development, as regressive because they attempted to provide adult males with the homosocial bonding and boyish freedoms of their preadolescence.

Probably the most in-depth, psychologically sensitive, and empirically based research on the participants in the men's movement by the mid-1990s was Schwalbe's (1996) sociological field study, conducted in or around a medium-sized city in the Southeastern United States. This study consisted of interviews of 21 men engaged in mythopoetic activity, participant observation at over 100 movement gatherings, and analysis of movement literature and tapes. The men that Schwalbe interviewed described their fathers as physically or emotionally absent, with one-third reporting that their fathers were alcoholic or abusive. These men also characterized themselves as "nice boys" in childhood, always trying to avoid angering others and always trying to please their mothers, who led them to believe that their fathers behaved badly because they were men. In adult life, these men lacked assertiveness vis-à-vis women, although they preferred women as friends, partly because they did not enjoy traditional male competition. Many of the men were involved in so-called twelve-step, or recovery, programs, mostly ones for adult children of alcoholics.

Regarding gender politics, Schwalbe (1996) found that the men that he studied tended to take feminist, especially radical feminist, criticism personally. While the men generally did not engage in "woman-bashing," he discerned much low-level unconscious sexism in their talk and behavior and a general disregard for women's issues and perspectives at the all-male gatherings. Also, the men tended to downplay the institutionalized power of men and to equate men's problems with women's oppression. Nonetheless, Schwalbe found that most of the men could be described as supporters of liberal feminist goals and as opponents of traditional gender role prescriptions. However, Schwalbe emphasized, these men were primarily concerned with individual, personal and psychotherapeutic change, not social or political change. They sought self-acceptance, knowledge of their repressed emotions, a validation of the male gender, and the warmth and support of male gatherings. Schwalbe observed that the relative material privileges that men as a group enjoy vis-à-vis women as a group have not spared the individual men that he studied serious psychological wounds, either in childhood, due to abuse, or in adulthood, due to failures to fulfill traditional masculine expectations.

In summary, this review of the literature on the mythopoetic men's movement through the mid-1990s found that social scientists and other scholars paid little attention to the subject. Journalists and feminist critics wrote most of the non-movement literature on the subject. Much of their work tended to be superficial, impressionistic, anecdotal, ill-informed, highly speculative, and sometimes not even very serious. The little scholarly research on the topic consisted mostly of feminist analysis and critique, usually from a sociological or historical approach. Although rich in insights and cogently argued, most of these feminist analyses lacked a strong empirical base to substantiate their debatable interpretations of the motivations of men who were active in the men's movement. Probably the most in-depth, psychologically sensitive, and empirically based research was Schwalbe's (1996) sociological study. However, this excellent study did not offer a broad analysis of the critical psychological, sociological, and historical factors that combined to give rise to the movement in the 1980s and early 1990s. The aim of this book is to offer such a psychosocial analysis.

Chapter 3:
The Crisis of Male Identity

Beginning in the 1970s, social scientists increasingly observed and commented on a crisis of male identity in the United States. In his social history of males in modern society, Stearns (1979) identified a crisis of masculinity, that is, "a sense that masculinity is sorely troubled in modern society, both in concept and in practice" (p. 1). Bell (1982) discerned a paradox of contemporary masculinity, in which "we are caught between old ways and new, between the era in which we grew up and the time in which we now live" (p. 3). Balswick (1988) argued that men were currently experiencing gender role strain because of the conflicting demands of the traditional male role and the modern male role. In her study of men's changing commitments to family and work, Gerson (1993) claimed that men had entered a "no man's land" in which no single road to manhood predominated for American men. Even the titles of books about men written by scholars during this period reflected this crisis of male identity: *A Man's Place: Masculinity in Transition* (Dubbert, 1979), *Men in Difficult Times: Masculinity Today and Tomorrow* (Lewis, 1981), and *The Changing Definition of Masculinity* (Franklin, 1984).

Key leaders of the mythopoetic men's movement suggested that the crisis of male identity and the men's movement arose mainly in response to problems that date back more than a century. In the PBS special *A Gathering of Men*, Bly speculated, "I think the grief that leads to the men's movement began maybe 140 years ago, when the Industrial Revolution began. It sent the father out of the house to work" (McCarthy & Ewing, 1990). In *King, Warrior, Magician, Lover*, Moore and Gillette (1990) attributed the crisis of masculinity in late 20th-century Western society to the preindustrial decline of male initiation rituals and to the ancient rule of patriarchy. While they also cited as factors the more recent breakdown of the traditional family and the concomitant absence of fathers, they implied that the origins of the crisis that the men's movement addresses lie primarily with centuries-old problems, not with contemporary developments. Bly was more explicit. At the very beginning of his interview in *A Gathering of Men*, he emphatically declared that the men's movement "isn't a reaction to the women's movement."

Such a perspective surely underestimated the magnitude of social changes that affected men's lives in the United States since the Second World War. It especially minimized the impact that the contemporary women's movement had since the late 1960s in challenging traditional gender roles, relations, and expectations. Certainly, a movement of men that arose in the 1980s, with the expressed aim of developing an alternative definition of masculinity, must have at least been in part a reaction, though not necessarily a hostile reaction, to feminism. Other postwar changes that affected men's lives and contributed to the crisis of male identity included the culture's promotion of a search for self-fulfillment, women's increasing employment, the sexual revolution, and, since the 1970s, economic crisis. All of these changes challenged the central feature of traditional masculinity—the male breadwinner ethic—which is the traditional standard, expectation, and ideal of the man providing financially for his wife and children to such an extent that they do not need to work to support themselves.

This analysis follows Ehrenreich's (1983) analysis, which viewed the postwar decline of the male breadwinner ethic as central to the social experience of contemporary American men. (However, most of the challenges to the male breadwinner ethic identified here are different from the ones that Ehrenreich discussed.) This perspective does not mean that the separation of fathers from sons does not pose a problem for male identity and did not contribute to the rise of the men's movement, as movement leaders claimed. Still, reference to this separation solely, or even mainly, cannot explain why the men's movement did not emerge until the 1980s. More recent developments must have been decisive. In order to understand and appreciate the impact of these developments on male identity, it is necessary first to review the social history of the central feature of traditional masculinity.

The Male Breadwinner Ethic

The historical origins of the male breadwinner ethic lied with the Industrial Revolution, which spread from England to the United States in the early 19th century. Before the Industrial Revolution, the male breadwinner ethic and the actual practice that it supported, that of the man being the exclusive provider, simply did not exist. In preindustrial American society, both men and women participated in economic production within the subsistent, self-sufficient household, whether on the rural farm or in the urban artisan and craft shop (Bell, 1981). Certainly, there was a strict division of labor based on gender, with men responsible for the crop, livestock, trades, and heavier labor, and women responsible for textile manufacture, garment manufacture, food processing, and healing (Ryan, 1975). Additionally, women were subject to the patriarchal rule of their fathers, then their husbands, and male domination in general, most importantly in the form of male ownership and control of most productive property. However, in spite of these divisions of labor and power, women's work was indispensable to the individual household economy. In her review of the male provider role, Bernard (1981) asserted, "In a subsistence economy in which husbands and wives ran farms, shops or businesses together, a man might be a good, steady worker, but the idea that he was *the* provider would hardly ring true" (p. 1).

The Industrial Revolution and the concomitant triumph of the capitalist market economy transformed these existing social relations. With the aid of the advanced technology of industry, a rising class of businessmen was eventually able to establish the dominance of the market over the economy by increasingly drawing—or driving—labor from the individual family-owned farm or shop into the more efficient or productive factory (Zaretsky, 1976). This economic transformation accelerated throughout the 19th century and continued into the 20th century. Before the Civil War, 88% of American men were farmers or self-employed businessmen, but by 1910 less than 33% of all American men were so employed (Kimmel, 1987). One of the most important consequences of the Industrial Revolution was that it split work life and family life—which previously had intersected in a single, unitary sphere—into separate public and private spheres, respectively (Ehrenreich & English, 1979).

This historically unprecedented split between family life and work life created the opening for the development of a novel ideology that assigned men and women to separate spheres. Between 1830 and 1860, powerful publishing firms in the Northeast constructed and transmitted to urban middle-class women a philosophy that promoted the relegation of women to the family and men to paid employment (Cott, 1977; Ehrenreich & English, 1979; Ryan, 1975). This "separate spheres" ideology held that the woman's natural calling was to nurture her children, provide a haven for her husband, and otherwise tend to home and hearth (Welter, 1966). Complimentarily, the 19th-century urban middle-class man was expected to work in the competitive market as a breadwinner for his family. Corresponding to the demands of their historically new spheres, women were characterized as being by nature emotional, dependent, cooperative, and altruistic, while man's nature was described as rational, independent, competitive, and self-interested (Cancian, 1987; Ehrenreich & English, 1979). This notion contrasts sharply with the reigning patriarchal ideology of preindustrial society that held that men were the noble sex, whereas women were selfish and base creatures who needed male moral guidance (Cott, 1979).

It can reasonably be estimated that men functioned as breadwinners for at least 80% of women not working in agriculture or in family businesses by the end of the 19th century. This estimate is based on the finding that only 20% of women, excluding those who worked on farms or in family businesses, worked in the paid labor force at this time (Kessler-Harris, 1981). Although nearly two-thirds of all Americans still lived on farms at the turn of the century (Hood, 1986), most urban families, working-class as well as middle-class, can be assumed to have lived in households that, in effect, conformed to the separate spheres ideal. Most urban women probably stayed at home not by choice, however, but by necessity. Full-time paid employment was simply incompatible with the objective demands of child care and housework, given the extreme length of the work day and the lack of child-care services and household labor-saving devices. It was logical from a strictly financial point of view for women, rather than men, to assume responsibility for the domestic work because, in the absence of reliable birth control methods and paid maternity leave, the biological facts and demands of fertility, pregnancy, and childbirth would already have reduced women's potential employment and earning power (Brenner & Ramas, 1984). Given the split between public and private spheres, such material factors were most likely the main reason for the relegation of men to paid employment and women to the home. However, the separate spheres ideology undoubtedly helped legitimize, reproduce, and thereby perpetuate this social practice.

Additionally, the male breadwinner role provided men with a source of masculine pride and self-esteem. Initially, men may have drawn on the breadwinner role to compensate for the disruptive effects of the Industrial Revolution, which diminished the main social base of male authority and identity in preindustrial society, namely, family-owned productive property (Stearns, 1990). As the United States continued to industrialize and urbanize through the 20th century, the male breadwinner ethic became even more pervasive and broadly supported as an ideal among both the middle class and the working class, even though the lower layers of the working class could not afford to support this ideal in practice. As society passed it down from one generation to the next, the male breadwinner ethic eventually came to be viewed as a tradition—the central feature of "traditional masculinity." Growing up in this culture, males internalized the male breadwinner ethic and defined their lives accordingly. Griswold (1993) explained the centrality of the breadwinner ethic to men's collective identity in the United States:

> Its obligations bind men across the boundaries of color and class, and shape their sense of self, manhood, and gender. Supported by law, affirmed by history, sanctioned by every element in society, male breadwinning has been synonymous with maturity, respectability, and masculinity (p. 2).

In the middle decades of the 20th century, the male breadwinner ethic survived important challenges to its dominance. In the 1930s, the Great Depression threw millions of men out of work and thereby deprived them of the means to support themselves and their families. During the Second World War, men abandoned their families and civilian jobs for the military front, and consequently women massively entered the work force to compensate for men's absence. Although the effects of the depression and the war on the male breadwinner ethic were direct, severe, and traumatic to both men and women, these two historical calamities were also discrete, temporary, and exceptional events that did not undermine the ethic's fundamental legitimacy or offer a permanent alternative to it. Indeed, after the war, employers summarily fired women workers to accommodate the returning veterans. Also, the government, the media, and professional experts promoted a *feminine mystique*—a conservative idealization of female domesticity—to restore and reinforce women's traditional roles as housewives and mothers (Friedan, 1963). In the late 1940s, century-old trends reversed, as the age for marriage and parenthood decreased, fertility increased, the divorce rate plummeted, and the percentage of never-married persons declined. The result was a "baby boom" and broad social support for the nuclear family ideal (Coontz, 1992).

Throughout the 1950s, popular culture and both public and expert opinion identified the meaning of manhood with breadwinning. In her review of the male breadwinner ethic during this decade, Ehrenreich (1983) observed, "If adult masculinity was indistinguishable from the breadwinner role, then it followed that the man who failed to achieve this role was either not fully adult or not fully masculine" (p. 20). A man's failure to marry and provide for his family in this period was readily perceived as a sign of homosexuality—a powerful and effective deterrent, given the culture's pervasive aversion and hostility to gay men (Griswold, 1993). The strong social sanctions against deviance from the male breadwinner ethic virtually guaranteed its status as the core feature of male identity in the United States in the conservative and conformist 1950s. However, the social changes that, in effect, challenged this ethic and thereby created the crisis of male identity that ultimately precipitated the rise of the men's movement also deepened during this period.

The Search for Self-fulfillment

The first major social change in the postwar era to challenge the male breadwinner ethic, though perhaps indirectly and inadvertently, was the culture's promotion of a search for self-fulfillment. The collective search for self-fulfillment represented a slow and gradual shift in the culture from an emphasis on commitment to traditional obligations to an emphasis on personal life and self-development. "Physical well-being, sexual amplitude, emotional intensity, and mental wholeness: these vague states were sought as ends in themselves," Clecak (1983) observed of the search for self-fulfillment (p. 145). This shift in American culture actually began in the late 19th century, but it accelerated greatly after the Second World War, especially in the 1960s and 1970s (Bardwick, 1979; Cancian, 1987; Yankelovich, 1981).

The roots of this cultural shift lied with three main factors (Cancian, 1987). The first factor was the increasing sense of material and physical security that Americans began to enjoy in the late 19th century. In the wake of increases in wages and leisure time, improvements in working conditions and housing, advances in medicine, and the general rise in living standards, Americans, especially middle-class and more affluent Americans, were more inclined to look beyond basic physical survival to higher-level concerns of life. The second factor was the growth of consumerism and advertising that accompanied the rise of consumer markets, especially during the historically unprecedented economic growth and prosperity of the postwar era. Consumerism and advertising promoted the spending of money and the buying of consumer items and counterposed a modern materialistic, hedonistic ethic of immediate gratification to the traditional puritanical ethic of thrift, self-denial, and postponement of gratification. The third social factor was the increase in the educational levels of the populace, as children were sent to free, mandatory public schools, and more people, at first the affluent, went to college in preparation for work in an increasingly complex industrial society. The rise in educational levels expanded self-understanding, fostered democratic and individualistic values, and thereby raised people's expectations for further self-development.

These social changes had a profound effect on the American character in the postwar era, especially during the 1960s and 1970s, when much of the conformism that marked the 1950s was seriously challenged. In their longitudinal study of Americans from 1957 to 1976, Veroff, Douvan, and Kulka (1981) detected a *psychological revolution*, represented by a movement from a socially integrated basis for well-being to a more personal basis for well-being. They found (1) a diminution of role standards as the basis for defining adjustment, (2) an increased focus on self-expression and self-direction, and (3) a shift in concern from social organization integration to interpersonal intimacy. The investigators observed, "Social organizations, social norms, the adaptation to and successful performance of social roles all seem to have lost some of their power to provide people with meaning, identity elements, satisfaction" (p. 17). They noted that men especially seemed to suffer a loss of meaning with the shift in cultural emphasis from social integration and role performance to interpersonal and individual sources of meaning. This pronounced difficulty for men would be expected because traditional masculinity is defined by an adherence to an instrumental achievement orientation best epitomized by breadwinning.

Surveys of the American public in the late 1970s reflected the cultural shift toward a search for self-fulfillment in the postwar era (Yankelovich, 1981). One survey found that 73% of Americans felt that they had more freedom of choice on how to live their lives than their parents did. Another survey found that a 56% majority of Americans no longer believed as their parents did that a man with a family has a responsibility to choose a job that pays the most over one that is more satisfying but pays less. The pollsters estimated that 80% of Americans were involved in the search for self-fulfillment to some degree, with 17% intensely involved.

Women's Increasing Employment

The second major social development that challenged the male breadwinner ethic was the increasing employment of women, especially married women. Unlike the search for self-fulfillment, which was implicit, indirect and inadvertent in its challenge, the increasing employment of married women clearly, directly, and undeniably contradicted the defining essence of the male breadwinner ethic. Beginning in the latter decades of the 19th century and continuing to this day, businesses increasingly and gradually drew women into the work force to meet the rising demand for labor, especially in clerical and sales positions, as the economy expanded. The long-term trend of decreasing fertility, the increasing enrollment of children in schools, and the advent of household labor-saving devices freed up women for these new job opportunities (Klein, 1984).

At the turn of the 19th century, only 20% of women not working in agriculture or family businesses were employed in the labor force (Blau & Ferber, 1986). By 1940, women's employment had risen to 27.9%. During the Second World War, that figure dramatically shot up to 36.5% in 1944, as women entered jobs to support their families and aid the war effort while men fought on the military front (Coontz, 1992). Although women's employment fell to 30.8% in 1947, due to the demobilization of women workers in the immediate aftermath of the war, it began to rise again at the end of that year, as women started to fill the new job openings in the ever-expanding service sector of the economy (Coontz, 1992). By the end of the 1950s, the decade of the celebrated feminine mystique, a full 40% of women were in the work force.

Most of the married women who sought paid employment in this period were working-class or lower-middle-class women who aimed to help their families attain the rising standard of living or maintain their relative class status (Bergmann, 1986). In the 1960s, college-educated, upper-middle-class wives increasingly entered the work force, not only for financial reasons, but for reasons of personal fulfillment as well (Van Horn, 1988). Beginning in the 1970s and continuing through the 1980s, married women increasingly worked outside the home to offset the rising cost of living and to help maintain their family's living standard in the face of inflation and economic crisis. By 1990, about 74% of women were in the paid work force (Gerson, 1993). Between 1950 and 1990, the percentage of married women who worked outside the home rose from 24% to 58%. In 1950, almost 60% of American households conformed to the traditional breadwinner/housewife arrangement, but by 1990 less than 14% did so.

Married women's increasing tendency to bring home a paycheck basically displaced their husbands' status as the sole and exclusive provider for the family. Griswold (1993) declared, "Nothing has posed a greater challenge to the ideology of male breadwinning and traditional male prerogatives than this transformation in the household economy" (p. 22). Although women's employment increased family income and reduced the burden of exclusive breadwinning on men, it nonetheless remained problematic for husbands overall. Certainly, women's increasing employment diminished a source of power that their husbands had over them, as women's independent income decreased their financial dependence on their husbands (Chafetz, 1990). Wives' employment also led to some husbands making greater contributions to housework and child care (Jump & Haas, 1987; Pleck, 1985). It additionally made wives less emotionally and physically available for their husbands, as they, too, were exhausted from work outside the home (Passick, 1990; Sherrod, 1987).

In a large, representative national survey, women's employment was found to be associated with depression and low self-esteem in husbands (Kessler & McRae, 1982). When it was determined that the husbands' depression and low self-esteem could not be attributed to increased domestic responsibilities or to the loss of financial power over their wives, the investigators speculated that it was related in some unspecified way to the men's traditional gender role orientation. In another national representative study, women's employment was found to be associated with lower job and life satisfaction of husbands (Staines, Pottic, & Fudge, 1986). After testing alternative hypotheses, the investigators concluded that the husbands' lower job and life satisfaction was due to "their feelings of being less adequate as breadwinners for their families" (p. 126).

The Sexual Revolution

The third major social development that challenged the male breadwinner ethic was the sexual revolution. Essentially, the sexual revolution consisted of a sexual liberalization, an expansion of sexual choice and diversity, and a relaxation of the traditional moral code that restricted sexual activity to heterosexual, monogamous marriage. This traditional moral code was unequally applied to the sexes, creating a double standard by which women were expected to guard their virginity against the sexual advances of their male pursuers. Before the sexual revolution, most women usually abstained from premarital sex, partly because they internalized the moral code, partly because they feared the threat of being stigmatized if they did not conform to this code, and partly because they aimed to withhold sex as a means to secure a marriage proposal and, thus, a promise of future economic security. After the sexual revolution, the partial erosion of the traditional double standard meant that women could consummate relationships with boyfriends and even engage in casual sex and suffer less social disapproval than in the more sexually conservative past. Beginning in the early decades of the twentieth century, the sexual revolution accelerated after the Second World War, especially in the 1960s and 1970s (Seidman, 1992).

At least three main factors facilitated the sexual revolution. First, the consumer culture encouraged the general loosening of self-restraint and publicly emphasized sex by using sexual imagery and messages in advertising to sell commodities (Freedman & D'Emilio, 1988). Second, the increasing employment of women enabled more social contacts between men and women, increased women's financial independence, and thereby decreased their incentive to withhold sex as a means to secure a marriage proposal (Reiss, 1990). Third, the marketing of the birth control pill in 1960—the most effective contraception to date—probably helped precipitate the reported rise in premarital sex in the 1960s and 1970s. In opinion surveys of representative samples of American adults, the percentage of respondents who viewed premarital sex as always wrong declined from 80% in 1963 to 30% in 1975 (Reiss, 1980). By the late 1970s, the number of women who reportedly had premarital sexual intercourse surpassed 80% (Reiss, 1990), up from 50% in the early 1950s (Kinsey, 1953).

For men, at least affluent men, the postwar prosperity and women's increasing tendency to say "yes" to sex fostered greater sexual opportunities and a new kind of lifestyle devoted to the pursuit of leisure, luxury, and libertine bachelorhood. Beginning in the mid-1950s, publisher Hugh Hefner and his *Playboy* magazine initially promoted this hedonistic lifestyle. Challenging the reigning sexual conservatism and pushing the limits of the unfolding sexual revolution, *Playboy* featured nude centerfolds of beautiful young women and warned men to avoid the "trap" of marriage and family and the burden of supporting a wife and children. Instead, men were encouraged to stay single and to have sex with as many women as they could attain, in casual encounters and temporary, nonbinding relationships, to maximize their pleasure and minimize their financial obligations. In the playboy philosophy, women were regarded as pleasure-giving and status-enhancing objects to be acquired and consumed, like the fancy sports car, the expensive hi-fi, the fine liquor, and other accouterment of the "swinging" bachelor. "The message, squeezed between luscious full-color photos and punctuated with female nipples, was simple," Ehrenreich (1983) observed of *Playboy*. "You can buy sex on a fee-for-service basis, so don't get caught up in a long-term contract" (p. 46).

Ehrenreich (1983) was exaggerating when she suggested that *Playboy* advocated prostitution as an alternative to marriage. However, the magazine certainly helped to articulate and popularize a view of women among men as prospective sexual partners who could be "bought" for the cost of a date. Such an attitude contrasted sharply with men's traditional view of women as prospective wives for whom they would provide for a life-time. Although only a small (but increasing) number of men would completely forgo marriage and remain bachelors for the rest of their lives, the playboy lifestyle and philosophy offered men in the postwar era an alternative version of male identity that dramatically deviated from the traditional breadwinner ethic.

The Feminist Movement

The fourth major challenge to the male breadwinner ethic since the Second World War was the contemporary feminist movement. Aiming to achieve full social, economic and political equality for women, the women's liberation movement that emerged in the late 1960s arose out of the changing social conditions of women, especially middle-class married women, in the postwar era. These conditions included women's increasing employment and educational levels and women's decreasing fertility rate—long-term trends that accelerated to an unprecedented degree after 1960, following their short-term reversal in the immediate postwar years (Chafetz, 1990; Klein, 1984). The main impetus for the rise of the feminist movement came from women's recognition of the discrimination that they faced in their new roles in higher education and paid employment, combined with their recognition of the irreconcilable contradiction between the feminine mystique and these new nontraditional roles.

Thus, a central task of the feminist movement was to affirm women's right to work outside the home and to oppose gender discrimination against women in education and paid employment. Indeed, one of the three demands of the first mass march for women's rights in the contemporary era, held in New York City in 1970, was for equal educational and employment opportunities, along with demands for the legalization of abortion and for government funding of child-care facilities (Klein, 1984). Feminists advocated equal pay for equal work, challenged men's monopoly on the highest paying, most prestigious and traditionally male jobs, and insisted that men and women equally share the burdens of child care and housework. Feminists also attacked men's sexual objectification of women in such institutions as beauty pageants, pornography, mainstream movies, television, and advertising, as well as in such interpersonal behaviors as rape and sexual harassment (Davis, 1990). Additionally, feminists proposed that both men and women transcend stereotypical gender socialization and embrace androgyny, which is characterized by a blending of those positive personality traits that the culture has designated as either masculine or feminine, e.g., masculine assertiveness and feminine sensitivity (Farrell, 1974; Fasteau, 1974). Men specifically were encouraged to embrace the feminist-inspired model of *the liberated man*, or the *new sensitive male*.

Despite the visible presence of organized conservative opposition to feminism, most public opinion polls and survey research indicated that the majority of men were generally supportive of the goal of women's equality. Furthermore, men became increasingly supportive over the years, and they became roughly as supportive (in terms of percentage of the population) as women, at least in their self-reports. In 1977, 60% of men, compared to 60% of women, approved of a married woman working outside the home, even if she has a husband capable of supporting her, and by 1988 that figure had risen to 80% of men and 78% of women (Niemi, Mueller, & Smith, 1989). During the same years, the percentage who believed that the traditional breadwinner/housewife arrangement was better for everyone declined from 68% of men and 62% of women to 45% of men and 39% of women. Between 1974 and 1988, the percentage who disagreed with the idea that women should take care of their homes and leave running the country up to men rose from 61% of men and 63% of women to 75% of men and 77% of women. Between 1975 and 1988, the percentage who supported the Equal Rights Amendment rose from 63% of men and 54% of women (*Gallup Opinion Index*, 1975a) to 69% of men and 76% of women (*Gallup Report*, 1988). Lastly, between 1975 and 1992, the percentage who supported the right of a woman to choose abortion, at least under certain circumstances, rose from 74% of men and 75% of women (*Gallup Opinion Index*, 1975b) to 83% of men and 83% of women (*Gallup Poll Monthly*, 1992a).

In spite of such formal support for women's equality in principle, or at an intellectual level, some evidence suggested that most men felt ambivalent about the changes that feminism demanded of them, especially in their interpersonal relations with women. In in-depth interviews of men affected by gender role change, Skjej and Rabkin (1981) found men to be cautiously supportive of feminism and opposed to economic discrimination against women, but divided over the issue of two-career families and concerned about feminism's potential to become repressive. The investigators also found men to feel distressed and estranged by the prospect of gender role change, to be reticient about women's demands for equality, and to have "just reacted, mostly in silent crisis. . . as if they were enduring an ordeal" (p. 12). Stearns (1990) concurred that "silence, not counterattack or acquiescence, has been men's most characteristic gender stance in recent years" (p. 172).

Other researchers found similarly complex responses of men to feminism. Based on interviews of over 300 men, Astrachan (1986) characterized men as falling into one of four ideal-typical categories of response to feminism: (1) opponents, (2) supporters, (3) ambivalents (the largest of the four groups), and (4) pragmatists, those who support women's equality to the extent that it eases the costs and burdens of the male role (e.g., women sharing the burden of breadwinning). Goode (1992) identified three common reactions of men to feminism: (1) surprise in response to the degree of women's anger; (2) feelings of hurt and betrayal in response to the charge that men have selfishly used their dominant position, which, they believe, they have rightfully earned; and (3) anger in response to the claim that men do not deserve any special deference from their wives for providing for them and bearing the burden of breadwinning. Goode asserted that the most important repercussion of the women's movement for men, in men's experience, was "a loss of centrality, a decline in the extent to which they are the center of attention" (p. 298). Additionally, Raphael (1988) perceived a "guilt-ridden reaction to feminism, with hypersensitive men apologizing profusely and confessing their insecurities aloud for all the world to hear" (p. ix). Raphael claimed that the appearance of the hypersensitive male, or "wimp," in the 1970s and the Rambo-styled "macho" man in the 1980s represented twin manifestations of male insecurity precipitated by feminism.

The Economic Crisis

The fifth and final major social development that challenged the male breadwinner ethic in the postwar era was the economic crisis that began in the early 1970s. Although this development was previously cited as one of several reasons for women's increasing employment, it needs to be discussed in its own right, as a direct challenge to men's financial ability to be the exclusive breadwinner for their families. Between 1950 and 1973, the United States enjoyed an historically unprecedented wave of prosperity, as the Gross National Product more than doubled and average family income doubled (Yankelovich, 1981). However, beginning in 1973, U.S. productivity began to slow down, and the postwar boom began to fade as the country faced the high cost of oil, the growth of the federal budget, and increased international corporate competition from its advanced capitalist rivals, especially West Germany and Japan.

Also, at this time, the postwar economic trend known as *deindustrialization* accelerated, as the manufacturing sector of the economy with its higher paying unionized jobs contracted, and the service sector of the economy with its lower paying jobs expanded correspondingly (Bluestone & Harrison, 1982; Burtless, 1990; Newman, 1988). Beginning with the 1974-75 recession and continuing through the 1980s, the U.S. economy became subjected to the unprecedented phenomenon of simultaneous unemployment and inflation, dubbed "stagflation." Showing a declining rate of profit, big business cut labor costs by laying off employees, by relocating production to other regions of the country or to other countries where the cost of labor was cheaper, and by union-busting. Faced with an increasingly antilabor climate, trade unions yielded to the pressures of management and agreed to concession contracts that bargained away employee gains in wages, benefits, and working conditions that had been won during more prosperous times (Goldfield, 1987).

The combined effect of these changes that constituted the economic crisis undermined the financial ability of men, middle-class and well as working-class, to be exclusive providers for their families. Between 1973 and 1993, men's average weekly earnings (adjusted for inflation) declined 14.3% (Griswold, 1993). Between 1976 and 1984, the median income for men who were sole breadwinners fell 22% (Gerson, 1993). Although family income rose 13% between 1970 and 1990, this increase was accomplished by the financial contribution of wives who increasingly sought paid employment. While the previous generation of men saw their income double from age 25 to 35, men who were 25 in 1973 saw their income rise only 16% in the next 10 years (Coontz, 1992). By the early 1980s, 72% of Americans polled agreed with the following statements: "We are fast coming to a turning point in our history. The land of plenty is becoming the land of want" (Yankelovich, 1981, p. 25). By the early 1990s, 74% expressed dissatisfaction with the opportunity for the next generation of Americans to live better than their parents (*Gallup Poll Monthly*, 1992b).

The Overall Effects

The combination of these five basic challenges to the male breadwinner ethic—the search for self-fulfillment, women's increasing employment, the sexual revolution, the feminist movement, and the economic crisis—diminished men's traditional commitment to women and children. In particular, the search for self-fulfillment, women's increasing employment (and consequently decreasing financial dependence on men), and the feminist movement created a moral climate that made it more socially acceptable for both men and women to end unhappy marriages. Thus, the divorce rate doubled between 1950 and 1985 and peaked between 1979 and 1981 in the United States (Gerson, 1993). In a study of a representative sample of American men between the ages of 18 and 49, Harris (1979) found that although 85% of men felt that family life is very important for a happy and satisfied life, 56% did not believe that having young children was a sufficient reason to postpone divorce, and only 35% believed that children are very important to the success of a marriage. Veroff, Douvan, and Kulka (1981) found that the number of fathers who had a positive orientation toward parenthood fell from 63% in 1957 to 49% in 1976.

Searching for self-fulfillment, seeking greater sexual opportunities, or attempting to avoid the increasingly costly role of the family breadwinner, men were steadily postponing marriage or in some cases rejecting it altogether. Thus, between 1970 and 1990, the percentage of men who were single rose from 8% to 17% (Gerson, 1993). In the Harris (1979) study of men, the investigators discerned a sector of men, an estimated 25% of the total, whom they described as individualistic, self-centered, and pleasure-oriented. Ehrenreich (1983) similarly identified a trend among men toward irresponsibility, self-indulgence, and an isolationist detachment from the claims of women and children—a flight from commitment. Concurring with Ehrenreich, Pleck (1987) also posited such a hedonistic trend but claimed that it was only one of three broad trends among contemporary men that also included traditionalism and egalitarianism. In another study of men's changing commitments to family and work, Gerson (1993) identified a sector of men with an "autonomous" orientation, who opt out of parenthood or significant parental involvement, in contrast to men with a "breadwinning" orientation and men with an "involved" orientation.

The increasing tendency of men to avoid commitment to women helped to fuel a wave of verbal attacks on men popularly known in the 1990s as "male-bashing." Distinct from simple feminist criticism of male privilege and male sexism, male-bashing here refers to the categorical vilification and denunciation of men. Fashionable in popular culture—in television, advertisements, cartoons, women's magazines, feminist literature, and miscellaneous gift shop merchandise—male-bashing included blanket characterizations of men as self-centered, inconsiderate, and insensitive (Farrell, 1986; Kammer, 1992; Kipnis, 1991; Morrow, 1994). Epitomizing this trend, Hallmark Cards' best-selling greeting card in 1991 announced, "Men are scum" (Kammer, 1992, p. 64). Furthermore, men were portrayed in absolute terms as victimizers who are psychologically and morally inferior to women, who are conversely portrayed as innocent victims (Goldberg, 1979; Gordon, 1982; Keen, 1991; Thomas, 1993). Some feminists held the entire male sex collectively responsible for such political evils as war and environmental destruction, as well as women's oppression. Speaking for many hurt and angry subjects of male-bashing, Keen (1991) complained that men are "being blamed for everything that has gone wrong since Adam ate the apple" (p. 206).

This generalized hostility toward men that was manifested in male-bashing probably had many different sources among women. Much of the hostility toward men came from women's heightened awareness of the legacy and ongoing experience of men's discrimination against women in the public sphere, especially in paid employment. Women were also angry at men for such acts of mistreatment and abuse as rape, battering, and sexual harassment. Women's hostility additionally followed from the simple recognition that almost all of the world's political and economic leaders (who really are responsible for so many of the world's problems) were, although only a tiny percentage of the male population, nonetheless male. Also, some of this hostility originated with the radical branch of feminism that viewed men *per se* as women's enemy (Koedt, Levine, & Rapone, 1973). However, perhaps most of the resentment that women felt toward men and that they expressed in male-bashing flowed from the hurts, disappointments, and frustrations that they experienced in their personal relationships with men. Women were discontented with men's seemingly limited abilities to be intimate, sensitive, supportive, and responsive to women's needs. Above all, women appeared to be especially bitter about men's continual failure to provide them with love and security, including financial security, in committed and lasting relationships.

Beginning in the 1970s, the escalation and convergence of the postwar challenges to the male breadwinner ethic, compounded by the consequent decline of male commitment and the corresponding appearance of male-bashing, produced a crisis of male identity in the contemporary United States. Bardwick (1979) explained that "when there is extraordinary value change, the security that people gain from conforming to the expectations of their culture is endangered and identity crises are predictable" (p. 22). From a psychoanalytic sociological perspective, the social changes represented by the five major postwar challenges to the male breadwinner ethic precipitated a collective experience of loss for men. Middle-class men were probably more likely than working-class men to have experienced such a sense of loss because the middle class was more directly affected by the postwar challenges to the male breadwinner ethic. Middle-class men were more affected by the search for self-fulfillment because of their higher income and educational levels, by women's increasing employment because of their wider support for the male breadwinner ethic in practice, by the sexual revolution because of their greater ability to afford the playboy lifestyle, and by the women's movement because of the middle-class base of feminism.

Certain age groups of men were also more inclined to have experienced the crisis of male identity. These changes especially represented a potential loss for the cohort of men who came of age amidst these changes but who were raised before their onset and who therefore had internalized the prevailing traditional standards and expectations for manhood. Thus, the baby-boomers, who were born and raised in the early postwar years and who were young adults in the 1970s, when all five postwar challenges to the male breadwinner ethic were present and converged, likely would have been most affected. Also, as already observed by others, men who entered midlife since the 1970s and who struggled with the particular issues of that developmental phase were more likely to have experienced this crisis of male identity very acutely. Additionally, the consequent confusion, ambiguity, and uncertainty about the meaning of manhood produced by these changes also created a potential crisis for young men who were raised in the absence of clear, consistent, and widely supported alternative standards and expectations.

Chapter 4:
The Problems of Father-Son Relationships

Before the contemporary crisis of male identity in the United States, most men uncritically supported the standards and expectations of traditional masculinity. Having internalized these socially transmitted values in childhood, men acted accordingly and thereby affirmed their identities, maintained their self-esteem, and provided themselves with a sense of security. They additionally received social approval from the rest of society, whose individual members also held these values. As long as it were possible for the masses of men to act upon such internalized standards and expectations and as long as they did so, the emotional gratification that they derived from the fulfillment of these values inhibited their ability to reflect critically upon and gain insight into their social conditions and commonly shared experiences. Therefore, most men would deny, minimize, suppress, or at least tolerate any problems or discontent which they experienced in connection to traditional masculinity.

However, in the 1970s, the postwar challenges to the male breadwinner ethic produced a crisis of male identity that disrupted men's adherence to traditional masculinity. As increasing numbers of men could not or would not act according to the male breadwinner ethic, many men subjectively experienced a violation of internalized values and, thus, a loss. This loss disinhibited men from their uncritical acceptance of their social conditions and commonly shared experiences as males. It enabled and motivated them to reflect critically upon and reevaluate certain features of traditional masculinity, especially those features which have been a source of strain for them. Two key features of traditional masculinity that many men have subjected to critical scrutiny are fathers' relative underinvolvement in childrearing and men's relative lack of emotional intimacy in interpersonal relationships, especially with each other.

The mythopoetic men's movement that emerged in the 1980s championed these grievances and made them the central concerns and focus of its activity. National spokesmen of the men's movement consistently identified the distance between fathers and sons and the distance between males in general as the primary problems of contemporary men (Bly, 1990; Douglass & Gillette, 1990). One national leader identified the father-son connection and male friendships as the two most important issues for men in the movement (Bliss, 1986). One local men's leader in Chicago identified fathers and male friendship as the "two pillars of men's work" (Baldauf, 1993). The participants in the Chicago men's movement that were interviewed in this study and whose perspectives will be presented in the last section of this chapter and in following chapters also attested to the importance of these issues.

Men's movement leaders generally attributed boys' needs to bond with their fathers and males' needs to bond with each other to innate psychobiological factors. However, it will be argued here, based on an integration of gender schema theory (Bem, 1993) and the empirical research findings on gender role conformity (Lamb, 1986), that the strength of these gender-based needs, although very real and very deep, is largely socially constructed. The male's special needs to bond with his father (or a father figure) and with other males flow from an interaction of three distinct but related developmental factors. These factors are the young boy's recognition that he is male like his father (or men), his experience of a positive relationship with his father (or his formation of a positive image of men), and his recognition of the (largely socially constructed) extent of the differences between males and females and the value placed upon these differences in his culture. The combination of these developmental experiences predisposes the boy to acquire the characteristics of masculinity as it is defined in his culture and to make himself in the image of other males. The boy then needs to bond with a father figure to receive support and validation in order to masculinize himself as such. Thereafter, the boy will experience a lifelong need to bond with other males, to be validated by them, and to share common experiences and pursue common interests together.

The more a culture differentiates between males and females by defining nonphysical characteristics as masculine or feminine, the more males will feel a special need to bond with each other. However, if they did not enjoy positive experiences with their fathers (or form positive images of men) in their early childhood, their feelings for other males and their own gender are likely to be complicated or conflicted, especially in a gender-polarizing society. Such ambivalence predisposes these males to diverge from the norms of conventional masculinity. While this predisposition toward gender role divergence increases the potential of these males to reject the harmful and restrictive aspects of conventional masculinity, it also tends to elicit social disapproval, rejection, and even these males' own self-devaluation. The contradiction of industrial society regarding male gender identity is that it alienates fathers from sons at the same time that it maintains a form of gender polarization. The alienation of fathers from sons impairs boys' abilities to form strong bonds with men and thereby conform to the particular norms of masculinity prescribed for them in industrial society. In order to show how this contradiction has caused males much strain, it will be necessary to review the social history of men's relationships with their sons in the transition of the United States from an agricultural society to an industrial society. (The issue of males' need to bond with each other will be examined in the following chapter.)

The Alienation of Fathers from Sons

The relative underinvolvement of American fathers in their sons' lives began with the Industrial Revolution. Prior to the Industrial Revolution, in the 17th and 18th centuries, fathers were very present and highly involved, both physically and emotionally, in the daily lives of their children, especially their sons. Fathers and sons worked side by side on the farms and in the urban artisan and craft shops in preindustrial society (Griswold, 1993; Rotundo, 1987; Stearns, 1990). Fathers taught their sons farming or the tools of the trade and eventually passed down a portion of their property to them, through the institutionalized practice of patrimony, so that sons could make a livelihood in the same way (Bell, 1981). In addition to preparing sons for their life's work, fathers were expected to teach their children religious and moral values, to teach them the rudiments of reading and writing, to supervise and discipline their children, and to oversee their courtships and marriages (Demos, 1982; Rotundo, 1987). Although fathers were the undisputed rulers of their families in this patriarchal society, mothers and fathers shared the emotional and coercive aspects of child rearing (Weinstein & Platt, 1969). While mothers were the primary caregivers of their children in infancy, parents considered boys their fathers' children and girls their mothers' children after age 3 (Rotundo, 1987).

So as not to romanticize or idealize the patriarchal past, it should be noted that many aspects of typical parent-child relations in preindustrial society would be considered extremely authoritarian and even abusive by contemporary, progressive standards. Despite the high level of daily, face-to-face interaction between fathers and sons, their relations have been described as formal, distant, emotionally restrained, and lacking in open warmth and affection (Rotundo, 1987). It was widely believed in colonial America that the expression of too much affection would ruin a child's character, especially if that child were a boy. Puritan parents viewed their offspring as the embodiments of guilt and sin whose wills needed to be broken through severe corporal punishment and intense psychological pressure (Mintz & Kellog, 1988). Before the advent of toys, children's games, or even the concept of children's special needs for play, parents treated their offspring as miniature adults and, thus, first and foremost as contributing producers in the individual household economy. It was common for parents to send their children at age 14 or earlier into the homes of strangers to be indentured servants or apprentices. Although many of these parental practices had declined by the late 18th century, under the influence of emerging individualistic and democratic ideals, American fatherhood on the eve of the Industrial Revolution hardly would have met the enlightened standards of affection, empathy, guidance, and nonphysical discipline that are advocated by contemporary proponents of nurturing fathers.

In spite of the authoritarian aspects of parenthood in preindustrial America, fathers were highly involved in the daily lives of their sons. Much as Robert Bly claimed, this state of affairs changed drastically for families who were directly affected by the Industrial Revolution (Griswold, 1993; Rotundo, 1987; Stearns, 1990). As the individual household economy was gradually displaced by the industrial capitalist market economy, men were correspondingly drawn out of their homes and into the offices and factories. Griswold (1993) elaborated on this development and its consequences for father-child relations:

> As the corporate household economy declined, more and more fathers became enmeshed in the world of competitive capitalism beyond the home. Rising numbers of men became commuters, shuttling between home and work. For those in the middle class, their destination might be an office in a bank or a place on the salesroom floor; for men of the working class, work might be in a small central shop or in a large factory. Regardless, urban and even town residents found that the bond that once united men with their children had been broken. Increasing numbers of men now spent their days away from home, engaged in

what became the defining characteristic of manhood for over a century: breadwinning (pp. 13-14).

The relegation of men to paid employment in the public sphere physically separated them from their children and thereby reduced the relative involvement of fathers in child rearing. The subsequent propagation of the male breadwinner ethic helped to legitimize, reinforce, and perpetuate this historically unprecedented separation of fathers from their children. The Industrial Revolution also undermined the influence of fathers by eroding the main social base of paternal authority in preindustrial society, individual productive property (Stearns, 1990). The decreasing ability of the increasingly propertyless fathers to provide patrimony to their sons greatly diminished the extent of their sons' economic dependence on them (Weinstein & Platt, 1969). Although sons remained financially dependent on their breadwinning fathers through childhood, they enjoyed the historically new opportunity as adults to break with their fathers and seek independent employment in the market. The individualistic ethic of the capitalist market, which fostered competition between men for jobs, money and status, strained father-son relations by encouraging sons to surpass their fathers occupationally.

Fathers were further alienated from their sons by the displacement of the father as the primary parent, beginning in the late 18th century. Under the influence of the European Enlightenment, innovative philosophers of child rearing rejected the patriarchal notion of children as embodiments of sin whose wills needed to be broken. Instead, they promoted the alternative idea that children were innocent and malleable creatures who could be shaped by the gentle discipline, moral persuasion, and reasoning of their mothers (Mintz & Kellogg, 1988). The 19th-century separate spheres ideology assigned primary child rearing of both boys and girls, both before and after age 3, to mothers and idealized their capacity for nurturance. Meanwhile, fathers were assigned a secondary parental role as the ultimate disciplinarian. Whereas child rearing literature in the 17th century and most of the 18th century generally directed advice to fathers and ignored mothers, the literature in the late 18th, the 19th, and the 20th centuries did the opposite (Griswold, 1993). This displacement of the father by the mother as the primary parent was reflected in the complete reversal of laws and court rulings regarding child custody disputes, from granting custody rights almost exclusively to fathers in the early 19th century to granting them almost exclusively to mothers a century later under the *tender years* doctrine (Stearns, 1990).

Another social development that eroded the influence of fathers (and parental authority generally) was the transfer of certain socialization functions from the family to the state and the professions. In the latter decades of the 19th century, an expanding, paternalistic government and emerging professional groups—including doctors, social workers, educators, and child-development experts—began to assume growing responsibility for the health, education, and general welfare of children (Lasch, 1977; Mintz & Kellog, 1988). The passage of legislation prohibiting child labor and instituting compulsory education curtailed fathers' control of their children's economic contribution to the family and substituted their traditional role as teachers of their children. The establishment of the Juvenile Court gave the government new powers to intervene into families, against the objections of parents, to institutionalize youth, not only lawbreakers, but also those who merely engaged in behaviors that offended Protestant, native-born, middle-class sensibilities (Coontz, 1992). Additionally, the proliferation of parent education, geared primarily toward mothers, fostered an ideal of perfect parenthood that inadvertently undermined parents', especially fathers', confidence in their abilities to perform the most basic functions of child rearing (Griswold, 1993; Lasch, 1977).

Another development that alienated fathers from sons was the strengthening of the adolescent peer group and the rise of the youth subculture. The removal of children from the process of production, particularly in the household economy, and the mandatory enrollment of children in schools qualitatively increased the influence of peers in children's lives—an influence that sometimes rivaled parental authority. Teenagers and young adults, such as college students, whose segregation from the world of work extended past adolescence, developed their own styles of language, dress, hair, music, and social rituals and mores. After the First World War, the mass marketing of the automobile gave youth a new freedom from adult supervision that greatly facilitated their differentiation from their parents. In the 1920s, the rise of consumer markets that catered to—and helped to create—the special needs of youth provided the material basis for the development of a distinct pleasure-oriented, commercialized youth subculture (Freedman & D'Emilio, 1988; Griswold, 1993). After the Second World War, this youth subculture mushroomed, and the "generation gap" widened amidst the expansion of these consumer markets, the rise in college enrollment, the explosion of rock'n'roll music, and the emergence of a counterculture in the late 1960s that rejected established authority.

Overlapping with and subsuming much of the youth subculture, modern mass culture is yet another feature of 20th-century industrial society that alienated fathers from sons. Modern mass culture was largely constructed out of the rise in general living standards and literacy rates, the growth of consumer markets and the advertising industry, and the proliferation of the commercial mass media, especially radio, cinema, and television. Mass culture promoted new technology, consumer products, fashions, and, above all, idealized images of youth (Ewen, 1976; Lasch, 1979). Just as industrialization and continuing technological innovation made the work-related knowledge, skills and techniques of past generations obsolete, so mass culture tended to make the values of the older generations—for example, thrift, hard work, self-denial, and sexual conservatism—appear quaint, outdated, and irrelevant. Mass culture also reflected and reinforced the relative decline of paternal influence that occurred in modern industrial society. Ehrenreich and English (1979) commented on the pathetic image of fathers portrayed in mass culture in the mid-20th century:

> Mass culture became obsessed with the diminution of the American male. In cartoons, the average male was shorter than his wife, who habitually entered the frame in curlers, wielding a rolling pin over her cowering husband. TV squeezed the American male's diminished sense of manhood for whatever laughs—or thrills—were left. The domesticated Dad, who was most hilarious when he tried to be manly and enterprising, was the butt of all the situation comedies. Danny Thomas, Ozzie Nelson, Robert Young, and (though not a father) Jackie Gleason in "The Honeymooners," were funny only as pint-sized caricatures of the patriarchs, frontiersmen, and adventurers who once defined American manhood (p. 240).

In the early postwar era, the alienation of fathers from their children became more defined among certain sectors, especially middle-class sectors, of American society. Professionals, managers, and businessmen in particular increasingly put in long hours at work to prove their loyalty to their companies or to gain a competitive edge in their respective fields (Rotundo, 1987). Also, postwar suburbanization meant that many fathers had to commute to work, which additionally lengthened their time away from home. Although women's employment rose overall in the 1950s, the propagation of the feminine mystique led many college-educated middle-class women to forgo professional careers and make careers out of motherhood and housekeeping instead—a development which inadvertently encouraged many suburban housewives who felt trapped and frustrated to live through their children (Bader & Philipson, 1980; Friedan, 1963). The growth of affluence and consumer markets further expanded women's traditional sphere of influence by enlarging their role as the household's main purchaser of consumer goods (Ehrenreich & English, 1979; Ewen, 1976; Friedan, 1963). While most middle-class men remained the head of the household as the primary or sole breadwinner, they were nonetheless largely uninvolved in much of their families' daily functioning, decision-making, and interactions. Feeling like outsiders in their own homes, many fathers passively withdrew from their children and deferred to their wives in most domestic matters, in which they as men generally had less interest, experience, or self-confidence in handling.

Despite the increasing disengagement of fathers in some middle-class homes in the early postwar era, in other homes fathers became more involved in child rearing. Indeed, there is evidence that fathers' involvement with their children began to increase in the 20th century overall after it initially decreased in the 19th century. Although the aforementioned factors mitigated against father-son closeness, countervailing factors outweighed the tendencies toward alienation to produce a net gain for paternal involvement in the 20th century. These factors included the increases in leisure time and the improvements in housing, which allowed fathers to interact more with their children (Stearns, 1990). Also, the growing legion of helping professionals encouraged paternal involvement in child rearing to supplement the primary care of mothers (Griswold, 1993). Especially after the Second World War, child experts promoted fathers' functions as playmates, "pals," and gender role models for their developing children (Ehrenreich & English, 1979; Griswold, 1993; Stearns, 1990). Researchers found that as early as the 1920s fathers were spending more time with their children, especially their sons, than their fathers had spent with them (Stearns, 1990). This trend increased after the Second

World War and accelerated in the wake of women's increasing employment and the rise of the feminist movement in the 1970s (Pleck, 1987).

Of course, the extent of fathers' increasing involvement with their children was limited by the aforementioned social developments that tended to alienate fathers from sons. Moreover, men's relative underinvolvement in child rearing, compared to the involvement of mothers, was consolidated and reinforced by subjective factors that built upon these objective forces and took on a life of their own. Growing up in a gender-polarizing society that assigned child care primarily or even exclusively to women and that in many ways alienated fathers from their children, boys observed and internalized the assumption that child care is a primarily or exclusively feminine activity. Therefore, males rejected child care and opportunities to develop their capacities for nurturance in order to satisfy the needs of their conventionally masculine identities and to gain social support. Additionally, men's rational self-interest in pursuing financial gain and status in the public world of work interfered with their emotional involvements in the family. The combination of these subjective factors, both emotional and rational, coupled with the objective factors, insured that men would not significantly challenge their alienation from their children.

The main purpose of identifying the social developments that alienated fathers from sons in industrial society is to show that the current relative underinvolvement of fathers in child rearing is not an inevitable product of human nature, but is a social construction that can potentially be transformed. Again, the intent is not to romanticize or idealize the patriarchal past or to justify reactionary calls for its restoration. Although all of these developments diminished the father-child bond, many of them were nonetheless highly progressive, at least in part. In spite of the great disruption and suffering that industrialization caused, it made possible major advances in science, medicine, and labor-saving technology, as well as the general increases in wealth and living standards. Also, the passage of legislation prohibiting child labor and instituting compulsory education protected children from exploitation by parents and employers and fostered children's intellectual and social development. Although the Juvenile Court tended to violate the civil liberties of youths and their parents and to uphold white middle-class biases, the Court's ostensibly rehabilitative stance toward young offenders represented an advance over treating minors in a strictly punitive fashion, as if they were hardened adult criminals. While professional experts surely undermined the confidence of parents, they also have provided them with genuine help and effective treatment in coping with the problems of children in a changing society. Despite their hedonistic, narcissistic and conformist excesses, both the youth culture and mass culture generally have promoted democratic values, technical innovation, and affirmation of individual needs. Lastly, all of these changes have had the liberatory effect of undermining patriarchal rule, which was so oppressive to women and children.

However, in spite of these progressive gains, the bond between fathers and children that was based on daily involvement in preindustrial society was lost. Although men were freed from the burdens of child care and were allowed to purse a materially privileged position vis-à-vis women in the public sphere, they were deprived of one of the potentially most emotionally satisfying experiences of mature adulthood—involved parenting. At the same time, children were deprived of close emotional involvement with their fathers. Although both sons and daughters suffered as a result, the consequences of the relative underinvolvment of fathers in child rearing were more problematic for boys, especially in a gender-polarizing society.

The Consequences of Paternal Underinvolvement

After the Second World War, sociologists, psychologists, and child-rearing experts became very concerned about the relative underinvolvement of fathers in child care, especially with their sons (Ehrenreich & English, 1979; Griswold, 1993). The experts focused on the family dynamics in which isolated suburban housewives raised their sons without the routine support of the boys' fathers, who put in long hours at work during the day. This particular familial context was viewed as aggravating the boy's already difficult developmental task of separating from his primary caregiver—his mother, a woman—to form a gender-based identification with his father and thereby establish a secure masculine identity. Therefore, the experts warned against the dangers of overinvolved and overprotective mothers, who supposedly emasculated their sons. The solution that the experts proposed to this problem was for fathers to become more involved with their sons and to function as their gender role models (Lamb, 1986).

Contemporary writers of men's issues in the 1980s and 1990s, some influenced by the mythopoetic men's movement, seemed to echo the child-rearing experts of the 1950s with their concerns about the consequences of the relative underinvolvement of fathers in child care. Lee (1991) identified the loss of the fathers that sons never had as "our deepest wound" (p. 3). Osherson (1986) asserted that "Boys grow into men with a wounded father within, a conflicted inner sense of masculinity rooted in men's experience of their fathers as rejecting, incompetent, or absent" (p. 4). Gordon (1989) claimed that paternal absence complicates the son's image of his father and his struggle to separate from him. Farmer (1991) argued that the father wound produces an aching father hunger that keeps the son from feeling his emotions fully, from separating from his mother definitively, and from grieving the loss of his remote father. Allen (1993) declared that the absence of father figures leaves boys stranded in a psychological "no man's land," where they feel uncertain and insecure about their masculinity (p. 49).

The empirical literature on paternal influence and paternal absence suggests that distant or nonexistent relationships between fathers and sons do put boys at risk for certain problems (Lamb, 1986). In correlational studies between paternal and filial characteristics, researchers found that fathers' warmth, closeness, and involvement are associated with competence and an achievement orientation in sons (Radin, 1982), with the psychosocial adjustment of sons (Adams, Milner, & Schrepf, 1984; Biller, 1971; Lamb, 1981), and with conformity to prevailing gender role standards of masculinity in sons (Mussen & Rutherford, 1963; Sears, Maccoby, & Levin, 1957). Conversely, sons with fathers who were cold, distant, uninvolved, or absent tended to be less competent and achievement-oriented, less psychosocially adjusted, and less masculine. Interestingly, the researchers did not find an association between paternal masculinity and filial masculinity, as warm and involved fathers tended to produce masculine sons, regardless of how masculine the fathers were themselves.

Lamb (1986) made two caveats about interpreting these empirical findings. One is that although differences in the areas of achievement, psychosocial adjustment, and gender role conformity were found between groups of boys growing up with involved fathers and groups of boys growing up with uninvolved fathers or without fathers, great heterogeneity existed within the groups. In other words, not every boy growing up with an uninvolved father or without a father experienced problems in all or any of these areas, and not every boy growing up with an involved father had no problems in these areas. The second caveat is that since these studies were correlational in nature, a causal link cannot be established between paternal characteristics and filial characteristics. Another factor or other factors that are correlated with the "father" factor may be responsible for the development of certain characteristics in sons or may mediate the effects of the father factor on sons. For example, the absence of adequate social support and the economic stress that typically characterize father-absent homes that are headed by single women, rather than the absence of the father in and of itself, may underlie the problems of boys in such homes.

A third caveat also seems to be in order regarding the implicit value that is placed on the filial characteristics that were measured in these studies. While there may be little contention over the relative value of an achievement orientation and psychosocial adjustment in sons, there is much controversy over the issue of gender role conformity. Since the 1970s, feminists, humanists, mental health professionals, gay rights activists, and, more recently, men's movement spokesmen have challenged the prevailing standards of masculinity, femininity, and gender role conformity. Millions of Americans who have been influenced by these groups and the great changes in gender relations and expectations since the Second World War also have found much fault with the rigidity, arbitrariness, and insensitivity to individual needs, inclinations, and potentials that characterize traditional gender expectations. At least among certain sectors of the population, there seems to be greater support for a flexibility or even an androgynous blending or selective enactment of aspects of roles that were traditionally designated as either exclusively feminine or masculine by the culture. Additionally, there is generally greater tolerance for divergence from traditional gender-based norms, at least in certain areas, in certain groups, and up to certain limits.

However, despite the much warranted criticism of traditional gender roles and despite growing tolerance for gender role divergence, it should be recognized that many aspects of traditional masculinity in males remain highly valued by most of society. These aspects of traditional masculinity include such characteristics as a masculine appearance and manner, exclusive heterosexuality, mental and physical strength and toughness, courage, independence, athletic ability, and an interest in stereotypically masculine activities, such as sports. Growing up in the culture, children internalize these social expectations and standards and express respect and admiration for those males who exhibit these characteristics. One need not value all or any of these characteristics in order to recognize that a boy who lacks them will likely experience certain problems. Specifically, such boys may face social disapproval and possible rejection, especially by male peers. They also may experience a conflict between their internalized social standards and expectations of masculinity and their perception or assessment of themselves as failing to live up to those values. Consequently, they are likely to feel anxiety, shame, and diminished self-esteem.

Participants' Perspectives on Their Fathers

In the first part of the interviews, the 10 men who participated in the mythopoetic men's movement and in this study were asked extensively about their relationships with their fathers and about other matters related to their childhood experiences. They were asked about their mothers, about parental discipline, about possible mental/physical/sexual/substance abuse in their families of origin, and about their peer relations while growing up. All 10 men seemed to respond very openly, candidly, and fluently to these highly personal and probing questions. However, only the most pertinent material relevant to the writer's main concerns are summarized, quoted from, and presented here. The names of the men have been changed, and most demographic information about them is not revealed in order to insure confidentiality.

One man, Adam, a small businessman-turned-counselor, recalled that he got along well with his father but did not have a close relationship with him. Adam and his father did not have a negative or adversarial relationship, as they did not argue and usually had good interactions with each other when they spent time together. However, Adam explained that his father's excessive devotion to work, in his capacity as a salesman and sole provider for the family, kept him away from his family. Although Adam believed that his father loved him and his siblings, he was disappointed that his father was not more emotionally demonstrative and involved:

> I'm not sure I ever remember him say "I love you," although I have good memories of my growing up experiences. . . . And he really didn't seem to have

much time to play with us kids or sit down and read to us or spend time with us. . . . There was nothing abusive. . . but there just wasn't the love, attention, affection, no efforts to make me or my brothers and sisters feel really wanted or special.

Adam concluded about his father, "He was probably typical of most men of his age and probably even most men even now. He didn't talk too much about his feelings."

A second man, Barry, a university professor, warmly recalled his childhood memories of his father coming home from work and playing games with him and his brother: "He was very sweet and willing to spend time with his kids." Barry said that his father treated him well, took him camping, had intelligent conversation with him at the dinner table, and taught him woodworking. However, despite such involvement, there was an emotional distance between father and son. Barry explained that his father had "hang-ups," in which he was unable to talk about certain sensitive subjects, such as sex, or to express or model feelings. This problem was compounded by the expectation that both parents placed on Barry to be "the super-intelligent golden boy who did no wrong and was somewhat perfect." Barry explained that his parents did not want to hear about or discuss any personal problems or conflicts that he may have been experiencing as he was growing up. Also, Barry disclosed that his mother dominated his father, who, he later realized, was "a lot like me—for a large part, listening, letting somebody else run things." An imposing figure with a very strong personality and white hair, his mother was once described by one of her coworkers as "the white-maned lioness." Barry likened his mother to his first wife, an abrasive, domineering woman, and he insightfully concluded, "I married my mother in some sense in the worst parts."

A third man, Carl, a commodity trader, described his father as wild, difficult to be around, irresponsible, and selfish when Carl was growing up. Following his parents' divorce, his relationship with his father worsened:

Up until that time I don't have a lot of conscious memories about us sharing special time together. I remember kind of watching and following and trying to stay out of the way. It wasn't as good as it should have been. When my parents were divorced, he remarried and kind of disappeared. He attempted to do the best that he could from a distance, being a distant father-kind of a surrogate father, but our relationship broke down.

Carl further explained that the problems related to his father's absence following his parents' divorce were compounded by his mother. Carl claimed that she spoke disparagingly of his father, tried to make Carl (the eldest son) replace his father emotionally, and consequently mentally "beat the little boy up all the time because her husband left her." Carl disclosed that he suspects that she may have abused him sexually as well, although he admitted that he did not recall any memories of sexual contact between the two of them. He stated that he hated women for a long period of time in his life because of his mother's mental abuse of him. He also reported that he had extramarital affairs with about a half-dozen women during his 13-year long marriage because "I was searching for the mom that I never had."

Don, the product manager at a company, described his father as cold, unloving, angry, verbally abusive, critical, and negative. He likened his relationship with his father when he was growing up to one "that you'd have with a next door neighbor that you didn't know very well and that you didn't like very well." Don elaborated:

> I don't think he or I liked each other a whole lot. We'd at least reached that point by the age of seven for me. We didn't have much of a relationship. There were moments that were sort of forced—like my mother would say, "Bill, you should take Don out fishing, or you should bring Don to do this, or teach him to play football.

Don rated his father compared to other fathers as a 3 on a 10-point scale (with 10 as the best), but on a more subjective scale he rated him as a 0 or 1. He explained that his mother played a contributing role in the conflict between father and son by standing between them and by forging a relationship with Don in which they functioned as each other's confidants and often devalued his father together. Additionally, Don further withdrew from his father when Don discovered that he himself was gay and that his father, a conservative fundamentalist Baptist, admired Anita Bryant for her antigay political campaign.

Ed, the director of business development at a firm, reported a very poor relationship with his father:

I didn't get along with him at all. I lived in constant fear of him my entire childhood. He had a very strong temper that didn't surface often, but when it did it was intense. Didn't physically abuse me—cracked me on the head a few times when I was younger, wasn't a physical abuse thing. But he had a very hard time getting close to me, and me to him. It was like when Dad walks in the door, everybody shuts up, just don't say anything.

Despite his claim that he was not physically abused, Ed reported that his father beat him up a half-dozen times in "very violent episodes" in which "he kicked me across the room." Although he denied that his father was an alcoholic, Ed's worst memory of his father is of him coming home drunk, screaming at Ed's mother, and Ed hiding in his room, scared. Ed attributed his father's aggression to the stress of dealing with Ed's mother, who had a psychotic break after her own father died. Despite his problems with his father, Ed stated that his biggest unresolved issue is with his mother, who mentally abused him with her delusions of religious persecution before she was institutionalized, when Ed was 5 years old.

Frank, a small businessman, said that he feared and hated his father when he was growing up. He recalled that his father worked compulsively and excessively, 12 hours a day, in order to fulfill his role as the sole breadwinner and to provide for his family of nine. Frank described his father as a "bad ass" authoritarian who disciplined his children but never showed them love or spent time with them. Frank elaborated about his father:

Growing up, he was probably very much like a traditional German. He was cold, very stern, very disciplined. Generally, he did actually show more emotion than my mother did. He was kind of hard to get along with. He was the kind of guy that came off and wallowed himself in self-pity. You know, "I've worked twelve hours a day, support you kids, and you don't appreciate it." The big thing with him was his kids didn't appreciate what they had. . . and so he always felt sorry for himself, like he had life so much tougher than everyone else.

Frank also reported significant problems with his mother. She was extremely possessive and dependent on him to the extent that she was jealous of the time that he spent with other people. Frank recalled, "My mother played the role pretty much that she would rather see me home depressed, but at home, than to see me out with my friends or another woman having fun." To this day, Frank declared, "She's the kind of person that if I went to visit her three times a week, she'd want four times. If I went four times, she'd want five times." Frank attributed his own possessiveness and irrational jealousy in romantic relationships to his experience of his mother's possessiveness of him.

Greg, an artist, described his father as an alcoholic and as authoritarian, rigid, quiet, and limited emotionally, though caring. He said that his relationship with him was strained, as his father usually lectured him, and Greg responded by challenging his authority. "I challenged his opinions, his beliefs about generally everything," Greg admitted. During his teen years, Greg would even go to the library to research a subject in order to prove his father wrong about a point over which they had argued. Greg also reported that his father whipped him with a belt once a week from the time when he was in the second or third grade until probably age 14. His father whipped him for such offenses as hitting his brothers or sassing his mother. Greg's mother aggravated the situation by threatening to have his father punish him when he returned home from work. When asked what kind of father his father was, Greg replied:

> If you asked me five years ago, I would have said he was a horrible father. Relative to the times and the culture that we lived in, I think he put a lot of energy into what he did. I don't think I benefited a lot from him while he was being my father. I see my father as a limited person who didn't think a lot about what he did and didn't try to acquire information about doing things better. He did things the way his father did them. I think the drawback to my father was he knew how to show affection to me up until I was eight years old, and then he didn't know how to show it to boys that were older than that. So I lacked affection from him as a father.

Harry, a corporate executive officer, described his father as a "very angry victim alcoholic," who was irresponsible and untrustworthy. Harry declared, "Basically, he was a victim act. He blamed everyone for all his problems." When he was sober, he was a very proud father, but when he was drunk he was very demeaning to Harry, as he would tell him that Harry was not worthy of his love. Many of the conflicts that the two had when his father was drunk escalated into physical confrontations, which included fist fights and destruction of furniture. Harry recalled the police bringing his father home because he was too drunk to drive. His mother tried to cover up for her husband and protect their standing in their small town community by telling Harry, "If the neighbors ask anything, everything is just fine." Some of the most painful memories that Harry had of his father is getting lost in a national forest on hunting trips when his father failed to meet him at a designated time and place after they initially separated to hunt by themselves. "I got lost several times because of his going elsewhere and drinking so that he was too fucked up to remember where he was," Harry explained. Harry commented on the limitations of his father and the traditional father role in general:

> I look at my father. I look at other people's fathers. You know, all I can basically see is they're there to provide, you know, a roof over the head, food, and whatnot, and the active insemination, if you will, for the propagation of whatever, that's it. To me, that's limited.

Ian, a salesman, had a father who was a rough man who was prone to violence, often got into physical fights, and walked with "a John Wayne type of stroll." He also was illiterate and a self-employed roofer who often traveled to get business. Consequently, Ian's father was often away, and when he did spend time with the family, he was not very verbal or emotionally expressive. Ian sadly recalled that his father never played catch with him, never took him to a baseball game, and did not interact much with him generally. However, Ian also remembered that he was once "the apple of his eye," when Ian was very young, before the birth of his three younger brothers increased the economic pressure on his father to travel more in order to get more work to support the family. Ian's father abused alcohol, and during his drunken binges he frequently battered Ian's mother. On one occasion, Ian intervened to shield his mother from being stabbed by his father. Although his father did not usually employ corporal punishment to discipline him, Ian cited one episode in which his father hit him and knocked him unconscious in response to his being arrested by the police for possession of marijuana. Despite such violence perpetrated by his father, one of Ian's most painful memories of his father is one of perceived neglect:

> I didn't have any guidance or parental guidance as to how to achieve, to do certain things. I was on a baseball team, Little League, when I was a kid. Nobody ever came to watch me play. Things like that which may not sound like a big deal. . .

> I remember when we went to get the uniforms the kids would get. Their fathers would be there to make sure they got a good uniform. I got the leftovers—this real big, baggy thing. I just basically felt like I was alone. And I had three younger brothers that I was basically a surrogate father for.

The last of the 10 men, Jim, a secretary, remembered his father initially as being very kind, tolerant, active, and involved with him. He fondly recalled his father playing pitch with him, dancing with him to jazz and Lawrence Welk music, and supportively escorting him down a long, dark hallway to the bathroom at night in order to allay his fears. However, Jim perceived a drastic change in his father's treatment of him between the ages of six and seven—a change that led him to conclude that his father really hated him. "He simply ceased to be a presence in my life as far as I knew. He was there, but he just wasn't *there*," he observed. Jim attributed his father's emotional withdrawal from him partly to his father's disappointment in his son's self-described effeminacy—specifically, his lack of athletic ability and interest in sports. Additionally, Jim identified other factors that he believed motivated his father's distance:

> I think things changed because it was expected. It was just a part of the culture, and also my dad grew up without a father... The way you behave with your sons after a certain age typically is not with visible affection and intimacy.... You didn't kiss your boys after a certain age. You didn't hug him. You didn't tuck him in after the age of six or seven. You just didn't do that.

Thus, all 10 men reported at least unsatisfactory, if not extremely negative, relationships with their fathers. Additionally, a majority of the men expressed serious grievances against their mothers. Given the extent of the problems with their parents, the first people with whom these men established interpersonal relationships, it might be expected that they would have experienced certain kinds of problems in their social adjustment while growing up, particularly with peers. Moreover, the empirical research literature suggests that boys who do not have positive relationships with their fathers are at risk for such problems (Lamb, 1986).

Indeed, one-half of the men appeared to have had problems in interpersonal relations with peers. Reflecting the social significance of gender role conformity, the five who did not have such problems all reported a high interest and involvement in sports, around which most young male friendships center. Carl, for example, reported that he made friends easily, had many friends, including some very close ones, and was constantly socializing with peers through sports. Ed also played sports, excelled at them, made many friends in the process, and was often a "ringleader" among a group of boys who got into mischief. Harry also excelled at sports, made many friends through athletics, and was very popular with both male and female peers. Greg, too, played sports avidly, made many friends in this way, although he made the qualification that none of his friendships were very deep. Ian said that he was initially shy with peers but that once he got to know them he became friends and played sports with them.

The men who did not have good peer relations while growing up presented various reasons for this problem. Barry said that he was a loner—shy, not outgoing, and not sociable—partly because he was negatively perceived as "the brain" by peers and partly because he avoided socializing with peers, as he feared failure and rejection, given his parents' failure to model interpersonal skills for him. Frank claimed that his friendships were not that good for a combination of reasons, including his low self-esteem related to his small size, his mother's not allowing him to bring friends over to their home (lest they make a mess), his working after school during his high school years, and his inability to fit smoothly into either the "jock" clique or the "freak" (drug-using) clique at school. Still, he reported that he made the friends that he did have through playing sports in the neighborhood. Adam said that he did not get along that well with male peers as a child because he was shy, did not play sports, dressed more nicely than other boys, got along better playing with girls, and generally did not fit in with other boys. Don also reported being a loner through much of childhood because of a lack of interest in sports, a greater interest in playing with girls, and a very poor training by his parents in social skills.

Lastly, Jim appeared to have had the most difficulty in peer relations while growing up. He claimed that he was rejected, verbally abused, and sometimes threatened and victimized for being artistic, unathletic, and effeminate. He reported that in junior high school a group of boys occasionally would surround him in the hallway and threaten to beat him up after school, although they never followed through on their threats. However, in his freshman year in high school, Jim was assaulted and humiliated when two senior bullies forcibly held him naked in the shower and pelted his crotch with soap while other boys looked on and laughed. When asked if he did anything to provoke or otherwise precipitate such a cruel attack, Jim replied, "What precipitated it was me, was innately me—and whatever they perceived to be my deficiencies or values that were in contradiction to theirs. I didn't fit. I did not fit. And that's very difficult."

In summary, most of the men interviewed in this study reported problems with their fathers, their mothers, and/or their male peers while growing up that are congruent with the psychosocial analysis of father-son relationships presented earlier in the chapter. All of the men reported relationships with their fathers that reflect the general alienation of fathers from sons in modern industrial American society. Of course, some of these relationships reflected more than mere alienation, as they included elements of mental and even physical abuse. Also, some of the men reported relationships with their mothers that reflected the tendency among mothers to become overinvolved with their children, given the culture's traditional idealization of their capacity for nurturance and its traditional devaluation of their other capacities. Lastly, half of the men reported problematic relations with male peers while growing up, as predicted by the research findings on boys lacking positive relationships with fathers. All of these findings suggest the possibility that the men interviewed here may have become involved in the men's movement partly because of problems rooted in childhood experiences with their fathers, mothers, and/or peers.

Chapter 5:
The Problems of Men's Relationships

The contemporary crisis of male identity has enabled and motivated men to reflect critically upon and reevaluate features of traditional male experience that have been a strain for them. As discussed in the previous chapter, one such feature has been fathers' relative underinvolvement in child rearing and the associated problems of father-son relationships. The alienation of fathers from sons in industrial society impaired boys' abilities to form strong bonds with men and thereby conform to the norms of conventional masculinity. Consequently, many males have grown up feeling a loss due to the absence or underinvolvement of their fathers and feeling insufficiently masculine or otherwise inadequate in a gender-polarizing culture. These problems of father-son relationships and consequent problems with male peers appear to have been contributing reasons for the involvement of at least some men in the mythopoetic men's movement.

    A second feature of traditional male experience that some men have reevaluated and that also appears to have been a reason for their involvement in the men's movement is the problems of men's relationships. These problems include both objective and subjective factors that interfere with men's potential to have emotionally fulfilling relationships with others, including other men. These problems impair men's ability to meet their innate human need for general social support and their largely socially constructed masculine need for male validation. In order to show how these problems developed, it will be necessary to review the social history of men's relationships. However, in a review of male friendships, Sherrod (1987) reported that a specific social history of men's relationships with each other in preindustrial America has yet to be written. A review of the literature since the time of Sherrod's report found that his statement still holds true of this writing. Nonetheless, it can reasonably be inferred, based on a general understanding of the differences between preindustrial society and industrial society, that many of the contemporary problems of men's relationships lie with the alienation of men from each other that developed in industrial society.

The Alienation of Men from Each Other

One of the developments in industrial society that impaired men's relationships and close social relationships generally was the growth of urbanization. The breakdown of traditional communities in small towns and rural villages and the growing concentration of the population in cities deprived an increasing number of people of the close-knit social support that the inhabitants of preindustrial society historically enjoyed (Wirth, 1938/1957). Urbanization tended to weaken the bonds of kinship, decrease the social significance of the neighborhood, and increase the number of impersonal contacts and interactions that people experienced in their everyday lives. With the increasing segmentation and specialization of people's roles, city dwellers became less dependent upon particular persons whom they knew fully and to whom they were emotionally close. "The contacts of the city may indeed be face to face, but they are nevertheless impersonal, superficial, transitory, and segmental," Wirth observed. "The reserve, the indifference, and the blasé outlook which urbanites manifest in their relationships may thus be regarded as devices for immunizing themselves against the personal claims and expectations of others" (p. 54). Wirth also noted, "The close living together and working together of individuals who have no sentimental and emotional ties foster a spirit of competition, aggrandizement, and mutual exploitation" (p. 56).

While this deficit in community feeling gave free reign to individual egoism in the city, the promotion of competition by free market forces and capitalist ideology further strained social relationships between men. As men were drawn off the land and out of the communal and rigidly hierarchical agrarian villages, they competed with each other for jobs, wealth, and social class status in the new individualistic society of social mobility and the "self-made" man (Miller, 1983; Rotundo, 1993; Sherrod, 1987). While ambition, combativeness, and competition were condemned in preindustrial America, they were endorsed as masculine virtues in 19th-century industrial America (Rotundo, 1993). Whereas boys and girls were not explicitly trained to different standards of character in preindustrial America, a new emphasis on a distinctively masculine emotional style characterized by toughness was promoted in 19th-century males. Stearns (1990) observed that "gentleness—a sense of yielding to emotion and a sensitivity to the emotions of others—was defined more exclusively as a female specialty than ever before" (p. 67). Stearns insightfully interpreted this cultural emphasis on a distinctive masculine personality as a psychological compensation for the crisis of male identity that occurred in response to the decline of family-owned productive property in the 19th century, in the wake of the Industrial Revolution.

This gender polarization of personality traits undoubtedly met such emotional needs. However, the different socialization of males and females to be tough and gentle, respectively, originated with the demands of the new gender-based division of labor, which identified men as breadwinners and women as caregivers. Weinstein and Platt (1969) discussed the socialization of 19th-century middle-class boys into emotional constriction, which was aimed at preparing them for achievement and success in the competitive market:

> The sons, therefore, were exhorted to develop self-control and self-discipline, to be self-observant, and to fear the loss of control stemming from emotional response. They were told that emotional expression, sentimentality, and sensuality were harmful (feminine) and that if they did not exercise self-control they would never become men. At home and at school the sons were urged to be industrious, calculating, and self-contained. The sons observed the controlled behavior of the parents, they identified with the active, competitive father, and they accepted the necessary restraints. It was thus possible for males to view personal feelings, even within the family, as obstacles to the achievement of the most important social goals (p. 179).

The rigid, emotionally constricted style of 19th-century males most likely would have limited their ability to be close to other people, including other males, and to meet their basic human needs for social support. It certainly would have impaired their capacity for direct intimacy—the sharing of vulnerable thoughts and feelings in close relationships. However, at the same time that males were socialized into emotional restraint, new opportunities were created that enabled them to bond with each other in all-male settings and thereby meet their specifically masculine needs for male validation. Although competition in the market economy divided men, the almost exclusively male urban workplace became the most widely shared site of male bonding, at least among coworkers and colleagues, if not between employers and employees. Dominated by the separate spheres ideology, 19th-century America also witnessed the growth of college fraternities, adult fraternal lodges and organizations, and such less formal institutions as taverns, barber shops, pool halls, and brothels, all of which fostered male solidarity and sociability (Pleck, 1976; Rotundo, 1993; Stearns, 1990). Perhaps the most enduring masculine institution to develop in the 19th century was organized sports—mainly football, baseball, basketball, and boxing, which remain a primary source of male bonding and sociability to this day, when men no longer dominate the workplace to the extent and in the way that they did a century ago.

In the 20th century, the dominant trend for men's relationships was away from other men and a separate male sphere. The main source of social support to which most men turned, largely at the expense of relationships with other men, was their private nuclear families, consisting simply of their wives, their children, and themselves. The elevation of private family life in men's lives was facilitated by increased leisure time and better housing and by the breakdown of traditional community ties (Stearns, 1990). Also, beginning in the 1920s, social scientists, helping professionals, and educators popularized a new conception of the urban middle-class family (now shorn of its preindustrial economic, educational, and welfare functions) as a source of romance, sexual fulfillment, and mutual companionship for married couples (Mintz & Kellogg, 1988). Eventually, the so-called companionate marriage and heterosexual love relationships generally came to be expected to meet almost all of men's emotional needs (Coontz, 1992; Pleck, 1976; Sherrod, 1987). Additionally, men were drawn closer to the nuclear family and away from relationships with other men by their playing a more active and participatory role with their children (Griswold, 1993; Rotundo, 1987; Stearns, 1990).

Another factor that alienated 20th-century men from each other was the spread of an intensified abhorrence of homosexuality. Before the 1880s, individual acts of sodomy were considered sinful deeds that should be punished, but the concept of homosexuals or a homosexual orientation and the stigma against them did not yet exist (Freedman & D'Emilio, 1988). Within the highly gender-segregated social life of 19th-century America, romantic and passionate friendships between unmarried young men (and between women) flourished and were socially accepted (Rotundo, 1993). These intimate male attachments did not involve any genital stimulation as far as can be determined, but they did entail affectionate touching, caressing, and kissing. However, in response to the visible emergence of a gay male subculture in urban centers in the 1880s, the medical profession, followed by other social institutions, postulated the existence of a homosexual condition and classified it as a sexual perversion. Once the general culture stigmatized homosexuality and introduced the notion that its presence or absence partly defined a person's identity, people became motivated to reject anything in themselves or others that might be perceived as a sign of its presence (Bem, 1993). The greater stigma against male homosexuality in particular led men to reject most physical affection and emotional intimacy between males in order to disassociate themselves definitively from this socially constructed threat to their masculinity (Nardi, 1992).

Men also may have withdrawn from close relationships with each other in the 20th century because they may have been in less need of such relationships than they were in the 19th century. Men's intensified heterosexual relationships with women may have met many if not most of their basic emotional needs for social support. Additionally, the decrease (though not disappearance) of gender polarization between males and females during this period probably diminished (though did not eliminate) males' largely socially constructed need for validation by other males. The main force underlying the decrease in gender polarization was the growing desegregation of males and females with the increasing entry of women into the work force. The workplace declined as a setting for male bonding, and men softened their tougher interpersonal style, partly to accommodate their gentler female coworkers (Stearns, 1990). Gender segregation also lessened with the spread of coeducational schooling after 1910 and the emergence of the unigender youth subculture of the 1920s. Also in the 1920s, parents began to moderate their differential gender socialization of their children, as they de-emphasized the importance of boys' ability to master fear and imposed new limits on boys' expression of anger. Stearns (1990) concluded that, consequently, "men are less preoccupied with differentiating themselves from women and finding ways to associate exclusively with other men than was the case a hundred years ago" (p. 155).

Contemporary Male Relationships

A review of the literature on contemporary men's relationships shows that there were significant differences between men's friendships and women's friendships. Overall, males and females reported similar numbers of same-gender friends—between three or four really close friends and between six and seven casual friends (Caldwell & Peplau, 1982). However, the quality of friendship differed between males and females. Males generally sought opportunities to share an activity, whereas females sought opportunities to share feelings (Brehm, 1985). Females tended to converse about topical matters (i.e., work and hobbies), relational matters (i.e., aspects of the friendship), and personal matters (i.e., one's thoughts and feelings), whereas males tended to converse about topical matters only, especially sports (Davidson & Duberman, 1982). Males tended to be less self-disclosing of their deeply personal thoughts and feelings to others, especially other males, regardless of age, region of the country, or social class (Fox, Gibbs, & Auerback, 1985; Hacker, 1981; Rotenberg, 1986; Sherrod, 1987). Also, married men were less self-disclosing to same-gender friends than were single men (Tschann, 1988). Lastly, men disclosed more about themselves to their closest female friend—usually a wife or a girlfriend—than to their closest male friend (Kamarovsky, 1974).

Although the historical roots of men's alienation from each other lie with the social developments previously discussed, the lack of direct intimacy in contemporary male friendships was perpetuated by a number of psychological factors. Certainly, one factor was the simple internalization of the social expectation that males maintain social distance from each other, at least in certain situations. Consequently, males would experience anxiety, diminished self-esteem, and fear of social disapproval if and when they violated this expectation. In particular, males may have been disinclined to share their intimate thoughts and feelings with their male peers because they did not want to be perceived as weak or feminine (Derlega & Berg, 1987; Douvan & Adelson, 1966; Williams, 1985). Males might have rejected self-disclosure and physical affection between each other especially because of their fear of being perceived as gay by others (O'Neill, 1982; Solomon, 1982). Additionally, there is some evidence from personality testing that suggests that males might have been wary about becoming close to each other because they perceived other men as threatening or potentially dangerous (Mazur & Olver, 1987).

Despite the lack of direct intimacy in male relationships, it should not be assumed that males were less interpersonally oriented than females. Although males generally were found to be less expressive of love, happiness, and sadness than females, relationships with loved ones and family were found to be as important to males as to females (Balswick, 1988). The lack of direct intimacy in male friendships masked a deep and covert closeness, vulnerability, and dependence that many males experienced with their buddies. In a discussion of the masculine interpersonal style, Sherrod (1987) explained, "When men are close, they achieve closeness through shared activities, and on the basis of shared activities, men infer intimacy simply because they are friends" (p. 222). Men seek companionship and commitment, not direct intimacy or self-disclosure, in their friendships with other men. Additionally, the kind of activities in which men typically engage, such as competitive games, offer them "comradery, pleasure, a sense of accomplishment, and an affirmation of masculinity" (Pasick, 1990, p. 114). Thus, in one respect, the focus on direct intimacy through verbal communication of personal thoughts and feelings may constitute a feminine bias that disregards the indirect intimacy and other benefits that males derive from shared activities.

Nonetheless, despite this feminine bias, there are genuine disadvantages to the lack of direct intimacy in men's relationships. Balswick (1988) asserted that so long as men do not verbally communicate their personal thoughts and feelings, they will be predisposed to psychosomatic problems due to unrelieved stress and pent-up emotions, that their self-awareness and understanding of their problems will be limited, and that their love relationships will not grow due to a lack of verbal reciprocity and mutuality. Pasick (1990) argued that the social expectation for males to suppress their tender feelings, such as feelings of sadness and grief, combined with the social approval of male aggression, will predispose men to channel these feelings into aggressive behaviors. Pasick also identified several other negative psychological consequences that follow from men's tendency to suppress their feelings, including decreased sensitivity to and intolerance of their own feelings and the feelings of others, overvaluation of rationality, avoidance of intimacy, the use of addictive substances to avoid unpleasant feelings, and the development of stress-related disorders. Sherrod (1987) observed that the indirect intimacy, or inferred intimacy, that typically characterizes male friendships is satisfactory and works well for most men until a disturbing problem arises that demands more direct emotional support.

Participants' Perspectives on Men's Problems

In the interviews conducted in this study, the men were asked to give their opinions of the main problems of men. All of them identified problems related to the socialization of males to be emotionally tough and self-sufficient and to refrain from expressing their feelings, especially their feelings of vulnerability. The men tended to focus specifically on the negative consequences of such personality socialization for men's relationships with others. Additionally, many of them identified the lack of established means for men to bond with each other in emotionally intimate, deep, and meaningful ways. All of the men discussed intrapsychic, interpersonal, or familial problems. They generally did not cite broader societal factors or issues.

Adam identified loneliness and isolation as the main problems of men. He asserted that men do not have a place to be open and honest with their life experiences. Often men lack love, support, nurturance, and an ability to have close relationships with others, especially other men. Adam elaborated:

> So many men, I think, have the impression that they have to be self-sufficient and be able to bear things by themselves. Maybe some of them can share at least some of these things with a woman, but otherwise they pretty much have to have a stiff upper lip and just take whatever comes along and deal with it by themselves.

Jim also identified emotional isolation and a corresponding narrow devotion to work as the main problems of men:

> Isolation, a very deep fear of loving other men, abandoning themselves to work, which, I think, ultimately is hollow, even if the work is exactly what they want to do. I think work by itself, only work, is meaningless. And I think men often—and increasingly women often—opt for that. They don't know what to do with their anger and hurt.

Ed stated that the main problem of men is their inability to accept their weaknesses and their feelings:

> Men have problems accepting their weaknesses, accepting the fact that they have emotions to deal with that are out of the traditional male context, the real old school: "Real men don't cry." "Real men don't do this or do that." And acceptance that there are feelings you have to deal with, that you have to address. . . . I think most men have a problem accepting their humanity, that they can feel pain, that they can feel joy, that they can feel sad and hurt, and that it's okay to show that. Conditioning the traditional male ego to be tough. You don't have to be tough all the time. You don't have to be right all the time.

Frank also identified the socialization of males to be emotionally tough as problematic. He said that men should not be afraid to express their vulnerable feelings, including with other men:

> I'm a total believer that men from an early stage are taught that they have to suck everything up. They are not allowed to express their feelings. Women are taught, it's okay to cry, it's okay to need people. Men are taught, you've go to be this macho bullshit, you got to be strong, you can't cry. The strength of a man is a man that's strong, doesn't cry, doesn't show any emotion. And I found through the Warriors that the opposite is true. The man who is able to express his feelings is a strong man, too.

Ian identified men's dysfunctional ways of expressing their feelings as the main problem of men:

> Unable to express emotions in an appropriate way. They do it through their substance abuse. They do it through their domestic violence. They do it through their lack of empathy for others, their inability to talk about what's real in terms of emotions—fear. I have brothers, you know, and I can't talk to them. It stays on the surface. They don't want to talk about that shit 'cause it hurts. That requires work.

Greg claimed that the main problems of men are their difficulties with emotional intimacy and their impaired relationships with their fathers, which he saw as interconnected:

> I think men—because of our poor upbringing and models from our fathers—we don't understand what it means to be intimate with either men or women. I think we act out of fear. We are sort of frozen by fear of getting close to people.

Harry stated that a lack of positive male role models is the main problem of men. He declared, "I think that all men are wounded because of the culture that we are now subjected to." He explained that "society doesn't have a very strong male focusing... My father didn't have a lot of friends. He had drinking buddies, but it's not the same." He added, "I don't think that men should be so tied up into the materialism, into the perks, or the frosting, if you will." Harry advocated that men, mainly fathers, should reject such materialism and strive to become positive role models for boys, specifically their sons, and demonstrate sensitivity and openness. He elaborated:

> I think a father should be very open and honest about his feelings and not swallow the—you know, basically hold them in. I think there should be a sensitivity in men out in the open. I don't think it's bad to cry. It's not unmanly or whatever.

Carl identified as the main problems of men their inability to share their experiences honestly with other men and the lack of an established, organized means for processing their personal problems and issues. Carl emphasized the need of men for emotional support from other men specifically:

> I think our culture makes it so that we confide in women, but we can't solve issues with women that are male issues because they don't have the ability to do it. It doesn't make them bad. They just don't have the ability.... Women don't have the answers that other men can offer.

Don stated that men, especially heterosexual men, are starved for male bonding. He contrasted the lack of emotional intimacy that he observed between straight male friends with the relatively deep and open relationships that he enjoyed with his platonic gay male friends. Don suggested that married suburban straight men in particular often do not have any friends, and much contact that they do have with other men is superficial: "They have a wife, and the other guys are sort of like the next door neighbor. 'Hi, Tom, how are you? How's the lawn? Looks great.'" Don concluded that the main problems of men are the following: "Not trusting one another, not listening to each other, not being open-minded enough to really try to understand where the other man is coming from."

While Jim held that men have a deep need to bond with other males, he observed that most men already meet their need for male bonding through sports and through conventional male friendships, despite their limitations. Therefore, he concluded, men in general are not as "wounded" as the men's movement claims:

> A large cut of men have either managed really very well with the conventions of our culture or are just so completely compatible with our culture that they don't get wounded—or not wounded very bad—or not badly enough to want to do something like this. I think a lot of men are quite comfortable and happy with the kinds of emotional connections men are usually allowed.

Similar to most of the men, Barry identified men's inability to feel, express, or name their feelings as the main problem of men. However, he went further than Jim in challenging men's movement thinking, in that he questioned the popular notion, which is so basic and central to the men's movement, that men have a special male or masculine need to separate from women and bond exclusively with each other. Following many feminists, Barry tentatively suggested that men may have a general human need, not a special male need, for social and emotional support from fellow human beings, whatever their gender. He also suggested that the men's movement might be contriving an artificial difference between men and women:

> They make a big deal about male initiation. It's not all clear to me how much of this stuff is dependent on the maleness and how much of it is human.... I don't know how much of it is that I've been pushed a line about minimizing differences between the sexes. And how much of it is, in order to make a community, they want to force a difference.

In contrast to Barry, Jim continuously reiterated men's special need to bond with each other. While he observed that most men satisfactorily meet this need in conventional ways, Jim stated that he believes that there are a substantial number of men who feel "this emptiness and this hunger" for emotional closeness to other men. He asserted, "It can't be fulfilled by women, no matter what your sexual orientation is. It can't be filled any other way." He elaborated:

For many men, there's a real aching void for other men. And I think men who are more conventionally trained and successful, they have other outlets for companionship. Sports, I think, provide an enormous link for men. And even though the emotion involved in it is not explicit—it's not stated—it serves the purpose: It forms those emotional and even erotic bonds. It serves men well. For those men who want something deeper or for those men for whom that serves nothing at all, the men's movement offers a place for us.

Chapter 6:
The Therapeutic Response of the Mythopoetic Men's Movement

In contemporary American society, men have struggled with the crisis of male identity, the problems of father-son relationships, and the problems of men's relationships. Although it did not identify itself as such, the mythopoetic men's movement represented a mass therapeutic response of men to these issues, with the purpose of exploring the meaning of manhood, reaffirming maleness, and developing an alternative definition of masculinity. A crucial element of the men's movement was the role played by its leadership in addressing these issues. In order to understand the role that the leadership played in this process, it is necessary first to discuss the psychosocial phenomenon of charisma.

Writing from a psychoanalytic sociological perspective, Camic (1987) defined charisma as "the central content of a relationship between (1) certain persons or objects and (2) individuals or groups of individuals who attribute something special (that is, what is termed 'charisma') to them" (p. 240). Camic explained that the precondition for the development of such a relationship is the subjective experience, on the part of the individuals, of extraordinary human needs. These extraordinary human needs flow from either socialization or loss experiences. Thus, individuals will be predisposed to attribute something special to certain leaders if they are socialized in such a way that they are unable to meet certain needs on their own or if they experience a loss that injures or overwhelms them to such a degree that they are unable to meet such needs on their own. The consequences of a charismatic relationship are that the individuals follow the leaders whom they experience as charismatic, and they either comply with or rebel against the existing order or value system, depending on the stance of the charismatic leaders.

Robert Bly and other leaders of the men's movement functioned as charismatic leaders for men, who collectively experienced a crisis of male identity in response to the loss produced by the postwar challenges to traditional masculinity, especially its central feature, the male breadwinner ethic. Leaders of the men's movement, including local staff who led movement activities and events, served as idealizable figures to help men cope with the crisis of male identity, the problems of father-son relationships, the problems of men's relationships, and various other personal problems. The leadership functioned in this way by offering an explanation of, and a solution to, these problems. The leadership explained that men had been wounded insofar as they had been deprived of close relationships with their fathers and of institutionalized initiation into the male community. Much of this explanation could be found in Bly's book *Iron John*. The leadership offered a solution to these problems—or a healing of these wounds—by providing a form of mass psychotherapy.

Bly's Book *Iron John*

Widely considered the bible of the mythopoetic men's movement, *Iron John* represented a major component of the movement's response to the problems of contemporary men. *Iron John* is a book-length development and elaboration of the ideas that Bly originally discussed in the landmark 1982 interview in *New Age* magazine (Bly, 1982). The bulk of the book consists of Bly's retelling and interpreting the Grimms' fairy tale "Iron Hans," which is about a young prince's initiation into manhood. *Iron John* remained on the *New York Times* hardcover best-seller list for 62 weeks and was, for that reason, probably that part of the men's movement with which the public was most familiar by the mid-1990s. It was certainly the most accessible, widely read, and influential piece of literature to come out of the men's movement.

In *Iron John*, Bly attempted to offer men a general understanding of masculinity and to provide them with metaphorical guidance in grappling with the problems that men face as men in contemporary American society. Although Bly dispensed insights throughout this rambling book, most of the key ideas and concepts that formed the basis of his philosophy and its appeal can be found in the preface and the first chapter (which is a rewriting of his 1982 interview). In the opening sentence of the book, Bly declared that "it is clear to men that the images of adult manhood given by the popular culture are worn out; a man can no longer depend on them" (p. ix). Thus, without identifying it as such or explaining its underlying causes, Bly alluded to the crisis of male identity, which inadvertently precipitated the rise of the men's movement and partly contributed to the success of his book. In the next sentence, Bly implicitly referred to the role of the midlife crisis when he informed the reader that by age 35 a man realizes that the received images of manhood are ineffective. Bly correctly observed, "Such a man is open to new visions of what a man is or could be" (p. ix).

The premise of *Iron John* is that fairy tales and myths offer men such "new visions" of manhood and masculinity. Bly argued that human beings stored in ancient stories the information that they need in order to adapt to new situations. He claimed that these ancient stories "amount to a reservoir where we can keep ways of responding that we can adopt when the conventional and current ways wear out" (p. xi). Bly likened the information contained in these stories to the information that is stored in the bird's instinctual brain for its survival, i.e., knowledge about nest-building, migrating, and mating. Bly asserted that these stories can be trusted because they have been subjected to "the scrutiny of generations of women and men" (p. 25). Most importantly, Bly claimed, these stories are an invaluable resource for men because they harbor distinctively male spiritual values.

Bly's offering of ancient stories as a solution to the crisis of male identity was appealing for a number of reasons. First, if the reader accepted the "bird" analogy and its underlying assumption that ancient stories necessarily provide naturally given solutions to contemporary problems, then the reader would have no more to do than simply heed the moral of these stories or, more specifically, Bly's interpretation of them. The legitimacy of the ancient stories was further bolstered by Bly's claim that they have been scrutinized over the generations, as if they represented some sort of refined product of humankind's efforts to determine universal truth. Actually, it is more likely that these stories had been uncritically transmitted from one generation to the next. Although they may, in fact, contain many insights into the human condition, they probably also reflected archaic values that were irrelevant at best and misleading and harmful at worst as guides in modern society. Lastly, the postulation of distinctively male spiritual values appealed to popular notions of essential gender differences and provided psychological compensation to men during the crisis of male identity in the gender-polarizing society of the United States since the 1970s.

Before introducing his model of manhood and masculinity gleaned from the "Iron Hans" fairy tale, Bly criticized and rejected two models of manhood that coexisted in contemporary America. The first model was the Fifties male. Bly described the Fifties male as a "macho" breadwinner who was hardworking, aggressive, nationalistic, emotionally constricted, and lacking in sensitivity and compassion. Bly observed, "Unless he has an enemy, he isn't sure that he is alive" (p. 1). Although Bly affirmed some unspecified qualities of the Fifties male (presumably his being hardworking and responsible to his family), Bly attacked his tendency toward domination and isolation. Bly's overall rejection of the Fifties male model likely appealed to contemporary men who had found traditional masculinity to be either an unrealistic or undesirable standard to fulfill in the wake of the postwar challenges to the male breadwinner ethic and the consequent crisis of male identity.

The second model that Bly criticized was the Sixties-Seventies man, or soft male. Bly claimed that this so-called soft male was a character type among contemporary men that developed as a reaction against the Vietnam War and as an accommodation to the feminist movement. Bly characterized the soft male as feminine-identified, thoughtful, gentle, sensitive, and nurturing, but lacking in energy, resolve, decisiveness, and fierceness. He also described the soft male as "life-preserving but not exactly life-giving" (p. 3) and as "a nice boy who pleases not only his mother but also the young woman he is living with" (p. 2). Although Bly did not explicitly label all American men soft males, he did assert that most men have been involved in the process of developing their feminine side since the early 1970s. While Bly affirmed aspects of this development (e.g., men writing poetry, appreciating nature, enjoying sex with the woman on top, and being empathic), he focused on and rejected this development's alleged tendency toward passivity. Thus, his critique of the soft male likely appealed to many men because it opposed passivity and a feminine identification in men, in line with traditional standards, while it supported sensitivity in men, in line with more contemporary standards.

Although Bly's vaguely liberal humanistic critique of the Fifties male seems basically sound, his analysis of the so-called soft male is questionable. Bly seemed to exaggerate the trend toward sensitivity among contemporary men. Certainly, the increasing employment of women pressured some men to assume more responsibility for child care and consequently to develop their capacity for nurturance. However, probably only a minority of men—mostly a certain progressive-minded sector of young, college-educated, middle-class men—consciously strove to fulfill the feminist-inspired ideal of male sensitivity that was characterized by a commitment to share domestic responsibilities equally and to give as much emotional support as they receive in intimate relationships. Also, even the specific examples of femininity that Bly affirmed in men, with the important exception of empathy, are mainly self-oriented in nature, not oriented toward others. Moreover, any trend toward sensitivity among men seemed to have been rivaled and perhaps even surpassed by a countervailing trend among men toward hedonism and an avoidance of commitment (Ehrenreich, 1983; Gerson, 1993; Pleck, 1987; Rotundo, 1987).

While generalized sensitivity among contemporary men is doubtful, it is even less clear that contemporary men became more passive. Some well-meaning men influenced by the antiwar and feminist movements might have overreacted to the aggression of the Vietnam War and to male domination by giving up all assertiveness, much as Bly suggested. However, such men would hardly have been representative of American men as a whole. Bly might have overgeneralized from such men, who might have been overrepresented among the unusual sample of men that he encountered in the milieu of poets, feminist spiritualists, New Age devotees, and other partisans of the counterculture. The possibility that Bly perceived men in this milieu as particularly passive is suggested by his observation that the young members of a New Mexico commune lacked resolve and the ability to say what they want (Bly, 1990). Such a perception is also suggested by Bly's hostile, rhetorical references to the "staff at the health food stores" (p. 12) and to "yogurt-eaters" (Faludi, 1991, p. 311).

Still, Bly might have been basically correct about there being a pronounced and widespread tendency toward passivity among contemporary men. It is possible that an increased prevalence in maternal overinvolvement and overprotection in some boys' lives in the era after the Second World War squelched their striving for individuation. Additionally, paternal underinvolvement in the postwar era might have weakened boys' development of the traditional masculine trait of assertiveness. Furthermore, the contemporary crisis of male identity might have undermined some men's self-confidence and their ability to assert themselves with women as boldly as they once did. However, it is also possible that Bly's postulation of increased passivity among men is simply not an accurate assessment at all. In his inability to transcend traditional gender stereotypes, Bly might have mistakenly perceived passivity where he saw sensitivity; or, in his admitted desire to break his ambivalent identification with his mother and women generally (Johnston, 1992), Bly might have falsely attributed passivity to sensitive men in order to rationalize rejecting the feminine-derived ideal of the sensitive male, which he renamed, somewhat pejoratively, the soft male. Whatever his reason and whatever the truth of the matter, Bly's postulation of a link between sensitivity and passivity in the Sixties-Seventies man allowed him to present his model of masculinity as a much needed alternative.

Bly (1990) declared that "the true radiant energy in the male does not hide in, reside in, or wait for us in the feminine realm, nor in the macho/John Wayne realm, but in the magnetic field of the deep masculine" (p. 8). This so-called deep masculinity is "incompatible with certain kinds of conventional tameness and niceness" and is characterized by "forceful action undertaken, not with cruelty, but with resolve" (p. 8). This deep masculinity is personified by the title character in the "Iron Hans" fairy tale—the Wild Man—"a large man covered with hair from head to foot," who lies at the bottom of a pond (p. 5). Distinct from the savage man, the Wild Man is simply a man who is "able to shout and say what he wants" (p. 26). Bly suggested that elements in every culture aim to "cage," or repress, this essential masculine force. In modern industrial society, the spirit of the Wild Man is at odds with the demands of corporations that "work to produce the sanitized, hairless, shallow man" (p. 6). Despite these societal pressures, Bly asserted, "When a contemporary man looks down into his psyche, he may, if conditions are right, find under the water of his soul, lying in an area no one has visited for a long time, an ancient hairy man" (p. 6). Bly claimed that the step that men need to make in the 1980s and 1990s is to begin the process of bucketing out their psychic waters to make contact with this inner Wild Man.

The main appeal of Bly's model of masculinity was, again, that it tapped into popular notions of essential gender differences and compensated psychologically for the crisis of male identity. It did this by identifying masculinity with characteristics that historically have been associated more with men than with women—i.e., forcefulness, wildness, determination, and body hair. Additionally, the images of a Wild Man lying at the bottom of a pond and being caged by society drew on certain well-known and widely accepted ideas of psychoanalysis, i.e., the unconscious and repression. Also, the reference to the "hairless, shallow man" of the corporation evoked the popular critique of the "organization man"—the 20th-century middle-class employee of a large corporation or government bureaucracy—who is a conformist that lacks the autonomy and individualism of the 19th-century entrepreneurs (Reisman, 1950; Whyte, 1956).

After introducing the model of the Wild Man, Bly devoted the rest of his book to a discussion of the young prince's experience of being initiated into manhood by Iron John (the Wild Man). Bly declared that the first step of male initiation is "a clean break from the mother" (p. 19). In the fairy tale, this break with the mother is symbolized by the prince stealing the key hidden under the queen's pillow—the key that will open the cage in which the Wild Man has been locked. Bly explained that the queen is the figure who possesses the key and thereby insures the Wild Man's imprisonment because the "mother's job is, after all, to civilize the boy..." (p. 11). Bly observed that the mother dreams at her pillow about her ambitions for her son: "'My son the doctor.' 'My son the Jungian analyst.' 'My son the Wall Street genius.' But very few mothers dream: 'My son the Wild Man'" (p. 11). If the son confronts the mother directly and demands her to let the Wild Man out, Bly claimed, the mother will reply seductively, "Come over and give Mommy a kiss" (p. 12). Bly emphasized that the son must steal the key because the "possessiveness that mothers typically exercise on sons—not to mention the possessiveness that fathers typically exercise on daughters—can never be underestimated" (p. 12).

This notion that the son needs to break with his mother likely appealed very much to the male readers of *Iron John*. In this gender-polarizing society, traits designated as masculine are highly valued in males, and it is widely believed that sons must separate from their mothers in order to develop them. However, the empirical research findings suggest that a warm relationship with the father—not a separation from the mother— leads to the development of such traits in the son (Lamb, 1986). Nonetheless, the specific cultural expectation that is placed on the boy to distance himself from his mother motivates him to do just that. Thus, the growing boy is likely to experience his primary bond with his mother and particularly her affection ("Give Mommy a kiss") as an obstacle to his masculine development, even though it generally is not. This is not to say that there really are not mothers who are overinvolved with their children—sons or daughters—in this culture which idealizes women's capacity for nurturance and devalues their other capacities. Although Bly overgeneralized from such mothers, his portrayal of mothers as typically possessive probably resonated with the experiences of many of his male readers, especially his middle-class, middle-aged ones, in the early 1990s. Such men were raised in the early postwar era of the feminine mystique, when many women chose full-time motherhood as a vocation and then lived through their sons ("My son the doctor") in order to fulfill their own frustrated needs for achievement.

Although Bly warned of the danger of maternal possessiveness, he mainly blamed fathers and other older men for boys' lack of initiation into the male community. "A clean break from the mother is crucial, but it's simply not happening," Bly lamented. "This doesn't mean that the women are doing something wrong: I think the problem is more that the older men are not really doing their job" (p. 19). Bly explained, "The boys in our culture have a continuing need for initiation into male spirit, but old men in general don't offer it" (p. 14). Bly elaborated that today initiation for the young man means helping him to remember and grieve his emotional wounds—including the wounds inflicted by "a remote father, an absent father, a workaholic father. . . a critical, judgmental father. . ." (p. 31). The young man must investigate or experience his wounds in the presence of an Iron John-like mentor, or "male mother" (p. 36). In the course of such initiation, the young man will learn "that nourishment does not come only from his mother, but also from men" (p. 15).

The appeal of these statements about male initiation likely were very powerful for male readers. For men who were struggling with the crisis of male identity, Bly offered a way to an ostensible "male spirit." For men whose fathers wounded them, Bly offered remembrance of their long-forgotten wounds, recognition of their pain, and an opportunity to grieve them. For men who simply never received nurturance from any older men, for reasons related to the demands of traditional masculinity, Bly offered the solution of the male mother—a strong, nurturing man—who is really the new sensitive male with a hairy chest!

A Form of Mass Psychotherapy

In addition to offering men *Iron John*, the leadership of the mythopoetic men's movement drew on the existing therapeutic culture to offer men a form of mass psychotherapy. This therapeutic culture essentially consists of those ideas, practices, groups, and institutions that are aimed at promoting personal growth, self-development, health, and cure, mainly through individual intervention. Related to the general search for self-fulfillment, the therapeutic culture flourished in the 20th-century United States amidst the rise in general living standards, leisure, and educational levels, and in the wake of the spread of individualistic and scientific ideas, particularly psychoanalytic ideas. These factors increasingly enabled people, especially the affluent classes, to focus on matters that transcend work, tradition, and mere physical survival. The therapeutic culture also thrived amidst the decline of community, tradition, religion, and shared meaning in the wake of industrialization, urbanization, suburbanization, and secularization (Cushman, 1990; Lasch, 1979). Despite the progressive aspects of these developments, the social breakdown that accompanied them created much social isolation and a crisis of meaning in people's lives.

After the First World War and increasingly so after the Second World War, this peculiar combination of rising affluence and social breakdown fueled the demand for psychotherapy. Indeed, psychotherapy addresses people's needs for self-development, social support, and meaning in their lives, as well as helps them deal with mental disorders and their unique personal problems and issues. This combination of rising affluence and social breakdown also facilitated the introspection upon which most psychotherapy is based. "Introspection intensified and deepened as people sought in themselves the only coherence, consistency, and unity capable of reconciling the fragmentation of social life," Zaretsky (1976) eloquently noted about individuals in modern society (p. 66). Rieff (1959) asserted that a new type of character emerged in the 20th century: the psychological man, who "lives by the ideal of insight—practical, experimental insight leading to the mastery of his own personality" (p. 365). Lasch (1979) elaborated on the plight of this so-called psychological man:

> Plagued by anxiety, depression, vague discontents, a sense of inner emptiness, the "psychological man" of the twentieth century seeks neither individual self-

aggrandizement nor spiritual transcendence but peace of mind, under conditions that increasingly militate against it. Therapists, not priests or popular preachers of self-help or models of success like the captains of industry, become his principal allies in the struggle for composure; he turns to them in the hope of achieving the modern equivalent of salvation, "mental health". . . (p. 42).

The growing inclination of affluent middle-class Americans in particular to seek out psychotherapy was additionally facilitated by shifts in the economy that fostered the kind of mental and interpersonal skills and characteristics that are conducive to psychotherapy. After the First World War, the economy and society became increasingly dominated by large bureaucracies—both corporate and government—that employed white-collar personnel, including managers, professionals, technicians, clerks, and secretaries (Stearns, 1990). In the 1920s, the number of blue-collar workers began to decline relative to the overall growth of the working class, while an increasing sector of the population was proletarianized with the decline of farmers and small businessmen (Zaretsky, 1976). Between 1900 and 1960, the percentage of the work force consisting of manual workers grew from 35.8% to 37.5%, while the percentage consisting of white-collar workers grew from 17.6% to 42% (Bell, 1973). During the same period, the percentage made up of farm workers declined from 37.5% to 7.9%. From 1947 to 1968, the percentage of the work force employed in the manufacturing sector decreased from 51% to 35.9%, while the percentage employed in the service sector increased from 49% to 64.1%.

These shifts in the economy shaped the expectations that were placed on the work force and even effected changes in standards and ideals of masculinity. Reflecting the demands of physical labor required in farming and in manufacturing, men in preindustrial society and in the stage of industrial society dominated by goods-producing were valued for being physically strong. In contrast, employees working in corporate and government bureaucracies, in the service sector of the economy, or in technical and professional fields are expected to develop their interpersonal skills and abilities. Such interpersonal skills as congeniality and thoughtfulness in particular are highly conducive to smooth collaboration in management and to good public relations in sales and office work (Brod, 1992; Pleck, 1976). Stearns (199) observed, "It became vital to teach men increasingly to emphasize what became known as 'people skills'—to interact pleasingly with fellow managers and subordinates, or with customers or clients" (p. 163). Commenting on this shift in work expectations that corresponded to the shift from goods to services in the economy, Reisman (1950) declared, "Today it is the 'softness' of men rather than the 'hardness' of material that calls on talent and opens new channels of sociability" (p. 127).

As early as the late 1950s, a full decade before feminists and humanists began to promote the ideal of the new sensitive male, Hacker (1957) discussed the new expectations on men to be emotionally expressive and interpersonally skilled. Hacker attributed these new burdens of masculinity, as she called them, to the work-related demands to ingratiate superiors and customers and to the growing emphasis on friendship between husband and wife in the companionate marriage. Hacker elaborated:

> As a man, men are now expected to demonstrate the manipulative skill in interpersonal relations formerly reserved for women under the headings of intuition, charm, tact, coquetry, womanly wile, et cetera. They are asked to bring patience, understanding, gentleness to their human dealings. . . . they must impress others with their warmth and sincerity (rather than as formerly with their courage and honesty and industry), they must be trouble shooters on all fronts (p. 229).

The manipulative aspect aside, these new expectations on men to be emotionally expressive and interpersonally skilled inadvertently prepared them for possible participation in psychotherapy. After the 1950s, these new expectations and the social conditions that produced the therapeutic culture accelerated, precipitating an explosion of psychotherapy. Leading the way were the loosely designated humanistic psychologists of the Human Potential Movement, who championed a variety of psychotherapies that generally rejected conformity in favor of self-fulfillment (Back, 1987; Bardwick, 1979; Clecak, 1983; Cushman, 1992; Ehrenreich & English, 1979; Wachtel, 1983). Starker (1989) commented on the array of psychotherapies that sprung up in the 1960s:

> Proponents of the new therapies offered a psychology for the masses, packaging their products for maximum appeal. They promised relief from pain, neurosis, and even ordinary unhappiness; they offered personal freedom and creativity by means of unbridled self-expression. It was time to "do your own thing," "become

a whole person," "get in touch with yourself," and "let it all hang out." This was the era of EST, Rebirthing, Primal Therapy, Co-Counseling, Sensitivity Training, Scream Therapy, Transactional Analysis, Bioenergetics, Encounter Groups, Rolfing, Gestalt Therapy, Nude Marathons, and so on (p. 113).

The strength and influence of psychotherapy and psychological ideas since the 1950s perhaps can be gleaned best by measures of growth of the field. In the early 1960s, only 14% of the public had ever used psychological services of any kind, but that number rose to over 26% in 1976 and to probably at least 33% by 1990 (Vanden Bos, Cummings, & DeLeon, 1992). Between 1960 and 1990, the number of members of the American Psychological Association rose from over 18,000 to over 37,000. In the mid-1980s, there were 159,000 psychotherapists in the United States, which represented an increase of over 100% since a 1975 estimate of 72,000. One observer contended that American society had become a "psychological society" by the late 1970s (Gross, 1978). Certainly, the public interest in introspection and self-fulfillment had generalized to the extent during this period that 72% of Americans reported spending a great deal of time thinking about themselves and their inner lives (Yankelovich, 1981).

The mythopoetic men's movement drew on, and was itself partly a product of, this therapeutic culture. Despite official claims to the contrary, the men's movement was, above all, a therapeutic movement that was primarily devoted to men's personal growth and self-development and to healing their psychological wounds. Indeed, Bliss (1992) described the focus of the mythopoetic men's weekends that he led as "recovery work, as well as discovery work. . ." (p. 95). In its promotional brochure, the New Warrior Training Adventure was billed as "a process of initiation and self-examination that is crucial to the development of a healthy and mature male self." The brochure explained that the New Warrior trainee confronts his *shadow*, which is, in Jungian psychology, the individual's unconscious part of himself that he does not want to be and that he does not recognize in himself (Kaufman, 1984). Techniques employed in men's gatherings at the Austin Men's Center included pushing, pulling, beating a pillow, pounding the earth, and screaming (Lee, 1991)—techniques which closely resemble Gestalt therapy *enactments*, in which the client puts feelings or thoughts into action (Simkin & Yontef, 1984). Additionally, the men's weekend retreats were similar to the weekend encounter groups of the late 1960s and early 1970s insofar as they aimed to establish immediate intimacy between strangers seeking personal growth and development.

Also, like most psychotherapy since the 1960s, the men's movement partly aimed (without usually describing it in these terms) to help men develop those parts of their personalities that the culture traditionally had designated as feminine and therefore stigmatized in men. These parts included their capacities for disclosing their intimate thoughts and feelings, for turning to others for support, for being sensitive and nurturing to others, for being physically affectionate with other males, and for crying when hurt or sad. Allen (1993) identified the development of the capacity for emotional intimacy in men as a key goal of Wildman Gatherings. The brochure of the New Warrior Training Adventure indicated that the characteristics promoted by the training included lovingness, gentleness, tolerance, and compassion. More explicitly, Lee (1991) declared that the men's movement is, among other things, "about finding, feeling, and taking back the feminine. . ." (p. 100). Thus, in one important and overriding aspect, the men's movement partly constituted an adaptation to the ideal of the new sensitive male that had been inadvertently fostered by shifts in the economy since the 1920s and consciously advocated by feminists, humanists, and psychotherapists since the late 1960s.

However, what distinguished the men's movement from other therapeutic endeavors was not its promotion of an implicit femininity in men. Rather, the distinguishing feature of the men's movement in this regard was its promotion of certain characteristics that traditionally had been designated—and that were explicitly and proudly designated by the men's movement—as masculine. These traditional masculine characteristics consisted of both substantial elements and stylistic elements. The substantial elements included such individual qualities as strength, courage, integrity, passion, vitality, assertiveness, a freer expression of anger, and the exercise of aggression when it is necessary and justified. The substantial elements of traditional masculinity also included such interpersonal elements as male bonding and initiation into the community of men. Thus, the brochure of the New Warrior Training Adventure indicated that the all-male training will make the man tough, wild, fierce, and passionate (in addition to the aforementioned traditionally feminine characteristics). The brochure described the training as a "process of moving away from the comforting embrace of the mother's feminine energy and safety into the masculine kingdom."

The men's movement also offered men stylistic elements of traditional masculinity. Many of these stylistic elements could be found in the props, activities, language, and surroundings of men's gatherings. More than simply reflecting men's style, these elements probably served a psychologically compensatory function insofar as they allayed men's anxiety about engaging in such stigmatized feminine activities as sharing intimate thoughts and feelings, hugging, and crying. Perhaps the prop for which the men's movement was most famous was the drum. Whatever other value the drum had as a musical instrument, the drum itself was an object that was strongly associated with masculinity because of its almost exclusive use by males in American culture. Another masculine element was the sweat lodge. Involving the gathering of nude or semi-nude men in an enclosed space that was gradually heated to high temperatures, the sweat lodge evoked the experience that most American males have had of sitting in a men's steam room or sauna. Still another element was the use of the word "warrior." Although in men's movement jargon the word "warrior" simply referred to the man's inner potential for strength and determination, it also evoked the image of one of the most quintessentially masculine figures in human history. Other elements were the location of weekend retreats in the woods or wilderness and the use of Native American rituals generally. Both of these elements evoked the image of a pure, natural, and primitive masculinity, uninhibited and uncontaminated by the demands of a modern, industrial, bureaucratic society.

Thus, the men's movement helped participants heal their psychological wounds and develop both those parts of their personalities that the culture had traditionally designated as either feminine or masculine, respectively. In other words, the men's movement helped men to become more psychologically whole human beings. In the next chapter, the 10 men interviewed for this study discussed how they as individuals were able to make these changes with the help of the New Warriors.

Chapter 7:
Participants' Perspectives on the Mythopoetic Men's Movement

All ten men who were interviewed for this study were asked to talk about their involvement and experiences in the mythopoetic men's movement, specifically in the New Warriors. They were asked how they learned of the New Warriors, why they decided to go on the weekend retreat, and what they gained from it, if anything. They also were asked about their most significant experience in the men's movement and what they think other men gain from the movement. Additionally, they were asked about their views on the all-male character of the weekend retreat and support groups. Lastly, they were asked to evaluate the New Warriors and their experiences in the men's movement generally.

Experiences in the Movement

Adam became involved in the mythopoetic men's movement following his divorce. After 28 years of marriage, his wife decided that she "needed to do for herself," which meant she no longer wanted to take care of her husband and their two children. Adam observed that his wife's decision to leave him was influenced by the fact that their friends were divorcing and by her involvement in a women's group, which was comprised of women who were either divorced, in the process of getting divorced, or simply angry at men. Adam explained that his wife's not loving him anymore was utterly devastating because he was very dependent on her and expected to be with her the rest of his life. "It felt like my whole life ended," he disclosed. Consequently, he entered psychotherapy, and his therapist eventually referred him to the Men's Room weekend retreat, another men's movement retreat in Chicago. Although Adam later became involved with the New Warriors, the most significant experience that he had in the men's movement was that first intensive experience with the Men's Room. Adam explained its impact on him:

> Literally, we went from being twenty total strangers to feeling like we would last friends for the rest of our lives. The weekend really nurtured being open and honest and giving nurturing to other men and receiving nurturing from other men, which most of us hadn't experienced a lot of. . . . I had experienced more intensity of love and nurturing and support in that weekend than maybe than I had

ever experienced before in my lifetime. It was like, you know, here I had spent my whole life looking for love and affirmation and affection because I hadn't really experienced that much of it at home growing up, and I spent most of my life trying to please people and make friends and do things to make people like me. And here I experienced all this intensity of love and support in this weekend that I'd probably been looking for all my life.

Adam further explained that the men's movement offered him opportunities to really relate with men, given that his life-long disinterest in traditional masculine interests made it difficult for him to relate to many men:

I have never felt like the typical man who was interested in sports. . . or cars, or money. You know, it seems like so many men, it's about the only things they can converse with one another about—cars, or what you do for a living, or sports, or women. With a lot of men, I've had a hard time relating. . . But with the men I've met in men's work, there's always the freedom to be open and honest and share what you're really thinking and feeling. And so, you know, it's a real contrast with what my experience with so many other men has been.

Jim also was referred to the New Warriors by his psychotherapist. He was seeing his therapist to deal with his life-long depression, his loneliness, and his growing isolation from everyone except his wife. Jim cited the lack of men in his life and his desire to overcome his fear of men as the main reasons for his decision to do the New Warrior retreat. He also disclosed that one reason that he participated in the Integration Group was the opportunity for close emotional contact with other men—contact that elicited, excited, and satisfied a homoerotic desire that he feels. Although Jim said that he was uncomfortable with this "undeniable sexual element," he indicated that the group vicariously met a need that he had long suppressed as a bisexual man who had never had sex with anyone but his wife. When asked what his most significant experience in the men's movement was, Jim replied:

I think seeing emotions displayed by other men. The emotional repertoire of most men is very limited. With me, particularly as an adult but also as a young man, I've cultivated an aloofness because I felt my emotions were so close to the surface all of the time that if I didn't practice detachment I would just be a mess on the street. So it was an interesting kind of a relief to see that there are other men who just want to sob and scream and all these other things that we are just never allowed to display—ever, ever, ever allowed to display. And with varying degrees of intensity, I saw that in other men. I'd never really seen that before.

When asked what he thought other men gained from the men's movement, Jim replied that it satisfied a special need of men to validate themselves as a distinct gender:

> There is something, at some intellectual level for some men, at a gut level for other men, at a mythical level for other men, there is something about being only with other men that can't be provided any other way. It confirms you in some way. It leaves you to think that, even if you don't understand yourself and your gender and your species, that possibly you could in the company of these like-minded men. There's just something that I've never been able to feel with a woman that I get from being with these men.

Greg sought out the New Warriors on his own initiative after hearing and reading about the men's movement. Before doing the weekend retreat, he had been in therapy—including individual, group, and couples therapy—for an estimated 4 years of his life. While in therapy, he addressed issues related to anger, intimacy, and his family of origin, primarily his father. When asked what his most significant experience in the men's movement was, he replied:

> The weekend was truly a profound experience for me. I gained a lot from the weekend. It was one of the most empowering things I've ever done. One of the things I didn't know I would get out of it—and it's really kind of lasted—is that it's made me tough. But it's a different kind of tough than what you'd typically think. It's not like football tough. It's like, I don't give up. So it feels lousy to do this. Do it anyway. It's important to do it. Whereas I tend to give up pretty easily. I used to throw in the towel if I didn't like the ways things were going.

Greg spoke very highly about his current Integration Group. He described the men in his group as three of his closest friends with whom he does not play sports. He said that they talk about such issues as their love relationships, parenting, balancing work and family life, and their goals. He sharply contrasted the openness that he experiences with men in his group to the superficial quality of his relations with other men.

"Essentially, there's not a censor," he explained about his Integration Group. "There's a switch that gets released when we're around each other that says we can talk about intimate things. We can share secrets freely. With other men, it's more of a surface kind of relationship." When asked what he thought the men's movement offers men in general, Greg replied:

> I think the men's movement is looking toward helping us to find—helping men to find—what the appropriate role is, both with other men and with women. I think it's also providing an outlet for us to deal with the source of the damage that many of us feel that we incurred, through the I-groups and the training experiences.

Frank was referred to the New Warriors by some-co-workers. He decided to try the weekend retreat because of his unresolved anger toward his parents, his destructive possessiveness and jealousy in romantic relationships, and his recurring bouts of panic attacks, for which he received much (unsuccessful) psychotherapy. Frank elaborated:

> One of the things that got me involved in the Warriors is that I really hated my parents. I felt that it was affecting my present life—my inability to carry on a relationship with a woman. So it finally got to a point where I was twenty-nine years old that something's got to change. And going through all these therapists. . . . I just found sitting around wasn't doing it for me—you know, two people talking wasn't doing it for me. And I needed something—and I really didn't know when I got in the Warriors it was going to be as intense as it was, but I really needed something like that. And what has really amazed me about the Warriors is that it's really after the root. And you take somebody like myself who, maybe after ten to fifteen years never cried, was sitting there crying. I had nights in the Warriors where I cried for three to four hours straight and was getting so much stuff that was so deep in me out of me. And the thing that's really impressed me about the Warriors is that it's the only outlet that I know of where you can express your feelings, totally express your feelings, regardless of what anybody thinks. You know you're going to get the support from your fellow brothers, your Warriors.

Don was referred to the New Warriors by his therapist. Don initially entered therapy when he was about 20 years old to address and ultimately come to terms with his being gay. Throughout his twenties, he periodically sought out psychotherapy to deal with several issues, including his parents, his sexuality, his fears, and his alcoholism. He additionally received help from Alcoholics Anonymous in battling his addiction to alcohol, which he described as "the salve that was nursing my wound." Also, Don said that he continuously sought out psychotherapy in an ongoing pursuit of growth, self-actualization, and personal happiness.

When asked what he liked about the New Warriors, Don replied that he admired their stress on "no bullshit," their honesty, and their attempt to make men into better fathers, sons, and bosses. He stated that the most significant experience that he had in the New Warriors was "digging down to the depths of my soul and baring it among other men and surviving." Don disclosed that at the "depths of my soul" he discovered fear, self-hatred, and shame. He specified that he suffered from "heterophobia"—which he defined as the anticipatory fear of heterosexual men discovering that he is gay and consequently rejecting him. Although Don apprehensively expected to encounter hostility or aversion from the overwhelmingly straight men at the weekend retreat, he happily reported that, on the contrary, the men there were very accepting and supportive of him and his sexual orientation. (Based on his impressions of men at various New Warrior gatherings and events, Don estimated that only 3 to 5% of the members are gay.) Don explained the major impact that this experience of acceptance by straight men had for him:

> It's been very good for me in that regard, breaking down virtually all of the fear with straight men. Are they going to like me: Are they not going to like me because I'm gay and they're straight? Are they going to think I'm coming on to them. A lot of those kinds of things have just vaporized in my life for the most part. I just don't care about that kind of stuff anymore. It was a huge block for me before.

Harry was referred to the New Warriors by his employer. Several years before doing the weekend retreat, Harry had received treatment for a cocaine addiction, which, along with his wife's cocaine addiction, helped to destroy their marriage and drain their finances. Harry spoke very highly of the New Warriors and his relationships with the men in his Integration Group. He explained that in his group, he feels loved unconditionally by other men, which is a rarity for him. He described the resulting feeling as "a wonderful non-narcotic feeling," a long-lasting "wonderful high" that is "euphoric." Harry discussed what he liked about the New Warriors:

> It takes layers off of me. I see myself in a lot of different people and watch how they go about it. I don't feel as alone as I did. There are other people that have the same hang-ups as I do. I also like the fact that I can do something to help someone. It also gives me a chance to be honored by other men. Sure, in sports you're being honored, but at the same time there's always people shooting at you anyway, you know, to knock you off. In athletics, it's not so much that it's team—it's winning is everything. Let's be honest here. It's not playing the game—it's winning. In Warriors, it's not that way.

Carl was referred to the New Warriors by his therapist. He had been in individual therapy for 7 or 8 years, including 4 years in which he went 3 times per week. While in therapy and drug rehabilitation, Carl overcame his cocaine addiction of 6 years, as well as dealt with his hatred of women and his generally destructive and impulsive behavior. During a bout of depression over the Christmas holidays, he decided to do the weekend retreat. At the retreat, Carl discovered that he was not the only man with serious psychological problems and that he could talk openly with other men, confide in other men, and not feel threatened by emotionally intimate relationships with other men. Carl explained what he liked about the New Warriors:

> I like what it did for me at that point in my life. I like the accomplishment that I felt from it. I like what doors it opened for me. And it gives me a sense of security, that if I really need something to fall back on, I have someone to go to that is a phone call away, that's willing to listen to my problems. . . . They're men there with open arms. That's a tremendous security for me as a man.

Ian was referred to the New Warriors by two friends. Ian had abused alcohol and other narcotics, including crack cocaine and heroin, beginning in his teens. After recovering with the help of Narcotics Anonymous, he realized that "I lost 20 years of my life." He decided to try the weekend retreat after experiencing the ordeal of a 6-week long "dry drunk." At the retreat, he worked primarily on his issues related to his conflictive relationship with his father and his unresolved grief over his father's death.

During the weekend, he gained "a temporary release" from the hurt underlying his drug addictions. When asked what he liked about the New Warriors, he replied:
> I like the opportunity to be open with what's really going on. You know, they talk about building that safe container to let somebody know who I am. 'Cause most the time, you're out there, and the question is, you know, "Who the fuck are you?" And the answer is, well, "I'm afraid to tell you." That's what I like about it.

Ed was referred to the New Warriors by his employer. At the time, he was extremely depressed, even suicidal, after his wife of 27 years left him. "When my wife left, I totally lost my mind," Ed declared. Prior to her leaving, Ed had abused alcohol for 20 years, drinking a quart of vodka every day during the worst period of his addiction. Ed reported that after getting married and having two children in his early twenties, he began to go out drinking with friends every night after work. He explained that he turned to corner bars as "a place to hide" from the economic burden of being the sole breadwinner for his family. When asked what he liked about the New Warriors, he replied that they helped him to examine his life, his patterns of behavior, and his underlying motives. "It gave me a panoramic view of my past that I would never have looked at in that way had I not been through the Warriors," he stated. Ed also disclosed that the "Warriors feed something in me that I'm really trying to wrestle with. But it makes me feel special, superior, like I'm different from everybody else, which is part of my shadow shit." He speculated that what other men gain from the New Warriors is "comradery, belonging, a sense of bonding, and a place to go where they feel safe."

Barry was referred to the New Warriors by a friend. He said that he was interested in the New Warriors because he recently had divorced his wife after she revealed to him that she was a lesbian. Although he was relieved that their unhappy marriage ended, he experienced a loss of emotional support because "she was the only person I talked to." He stated that he had no close friends and that he needed to build some relationships with men. When asked what his most significant experience with the New Warriors was, Barry replied, "Being exposed to all these people being honest to their emotional roots. It was a totally different environment, situation. And things that I'd been hiding and didn't want to deal with, I saw in a mirror." Despite this growth-producing experience, Barry expressed frustration over how little his newfound self-awareness had translated into real behavioral and personality change. He also disclosed that the men in his Integration Group are important to him but that he is still reasonably distant from them. He suggested that part of his problem in relating to the other men is his tendency to "go to my head," that is, to relate at a more cognitive or intellectual level rather than at an emotional level.

Views on the All-Male Gatherings

After being asked about their experiences in the mythopoetic men's movement, the men were asked about how important it was that the weekend retreat and follow-up Integration Groups be limited to men. Most men replied that it was very important that the retreat and support groups be all-male, and they gave various reasons for this general position. For example, although Adam recognized the value of therapy groups with both men and women, he defended the need for all-male groups in the men's movement:

> Yeah, definitely, there's a time and place for groups for just men because there's a tendency on the part of we men when there are women in the group, first of all, to not be entirely honest. We want to make a good impression, and there's a part of us that wants to portray the macho image. And there's a certain amount of sexual stuff, feelings that go on.

Jim stated that it was essential that the men's movement groups remain all-male:

> I would never, never do this if women were present. That's because what I'm getting out of this is only something that men can provide. They can only provide validation that stems organically from their own experience as men, whether it's their experience as effeminate men (as my case), whether its their experience as macho men, men in between, or men who have had everything go right in life. The only way I can have the kind of validation that organically I seem to crave is by having that come from other men.

Carl also defended the all-male character of the groups, claiming that both sexes need to meet separately first before they can meet together in mixed groups:

> Everybody has to be willing to open up. Most people don't know how to do that, don't have the ability to do it. If you're in a group of men, they have a tendency to open up more. I have been around women that enhance men's ability to open

up and help them with other issues. I believe that you can take—could take—Warrior men and women that have had individual exposures and put them together and really use that synergy to open the whole thing up and get to issues more effectively. But you have to do this one first and this one first to get that. Because men need to become confident among themselves. Women need to become confident among themselves.

Don also stated that it was very important that the groups be limited to men. He said that if women were present, he would feel inhibited to talk about sexual issues graphically, to disclose his acts of sexual infidelity, to use crude language, or "to just be a guy, doing a guy thing—farting, whatever." Don also stated that he would not trust women to respect the confidentiality of the groups. Additionally, he argued that gender differences would make mixed groups unfeasible:

It's extremely important that the groups be all-male. The fact that it is all-male definitely allows for discussion of issues on a much deeper level than would be possible if women were present. There's a definite difference between men and women anyhow in the way we're socialized. . . . Women think differently than men. Men think differently than women—and relate in different types of ways. Women are more nurturing by nature, usually by socialization or nature, whatever. They tend to hang out together and tell little secrets about each other. Guys don't do that. A lot of things are different. It actually would not work, and I would not even participate in it.

Ian stated that he prefers that the groups be all-male because of the general security that this condition provides him and because of the particular issues that he shares in the groups. He also disclosed that he values the newfound emotional intimacy with other men, which he never experienced with his father or the drug addicts with whom he socialized. Ian facetiously observed, "You don't stick a needle in your arm and turn around and start talking about feelings with the guy next to you." He also explained that the presence of women would inhibit his ability to share with the group:

I don't know how much I would disclose if there were women there. Some of my issues revolve around how I get along with women. I need to be very blunt and open about that. Another man, being a male, may have had or may understand those difficulties, whereas a woman may have been a victim of those difficulties. I don't know how far I could go if women were involved.

Although they were not as verbal in addressing this issue as the five men already presented, the other five men also expressed their views on the "all-male" issue. Harry stated that he valued the all-male character of his Integration Group because "there's no bullshit" and because he would not talk about certain issues, for example, sexual matters, if women were present. Frank also said that men would not express themselves as openly if women were present because men would be too concerned about what women think of them, especially if they are sharing angry feelings toward mothers or girlfriends. Greg claimed that men are able to talk about their vulnerabilities and their experiences with men in an all-male group in a way that they would not be able to do if women were present. Diverging from the majority viewpoint, Ed stated that he would like to see women admitted to the Integration Groups: "I really sincerely feel that to get the proper balance of life, we're not out there dealing only with men the whole fucking day. I want to hear a woman's point of view on issues we talk about in the I-Group." Lastly, while he acknowledged that it is easier for men to talk about their sexual problems in all-male groups, Barry questioned the overriding importance that the New Warriors attribute to the all-male character of the groups, and again he suggested that the men's movement may be erecting an artificial boundary between men and women.

Evaluations of the Movement

The men were asked to discuss how their involvement in the mythopoetic men's movement has affected their lives. Almost all of the men reported significant, positive change in their lives as a result of their involvement. Adam replied, "I'd say it has transformed my life." In support of this statement, he cited improvements in his self-image, self-confidence, interpersonal skills, and general relatedness to others. He further explained that his involvement in the men's movement inspired him to go back to school and get his Master's degree in order to change careers and become a counselor. Barry disclosed that his work with the New Warriors has helped him become aware of his own feelings, to be more understanding of others' feelings, and to attend to the emotional aspect as well as the cognitive aspect of interpersonal communication, especially in his family. Carl disclosed that his experience with the New Warriors has enabled him to look critically at himself, to turn to other men for emotional support, to make better decisions in taking care of himself, and to become closer to his long-estranged father. Don replied that his experience has allowed him to commit more to other people, especially other men, and to develop strong relationships with heterosexual men.

The other men had similar glowing reports of their experiences. Frank said that his experience has led him to become less materialistic, to value friendship more, and to overcome his fear of expressing his intimate feelings. Greg responded that because of his experience he is a more nurturing, androgynous, and less role-oriented parent, and he is more easily intimate with men whom he perceives as open to such intimacy. Stating that joining the New Warriors was "the single most important thing I've done for myself," Harry shared that his involvement enabled him to confront and then forgive and thereby get closer to his father. He added that he has learned to listen more, not to speak out so quickly, and to accept and enjoy hugging other men. Ian claimed that his experience has empowered him to tell people what he needs from them, to be more direct about his feelings, and to sustain a romantic relationship with a woman to whom he is engaged to marry. In contrast, Jim stated that he both doubts and envies men who claim that their involvement in the men's movement changed their lives, as he perceives the changes that he has made to be very small. However, he acknowledged that his involvement galvanized him to go back to school to get his Bachelor's degree and that he now feels less socially isolated than he did before.

The man who described the greatest variety of changes in his life as a result of his involvement in the New Warriors was Ed. He explained:

> By and large, I think it's had a very positive effect on my life. It's helped me get through what's been the most difficult part of my life. It's still ongoing. I think that I've been able to say things to my estranged wife that I've never thought I'd be able to say. I think it's brought me to a personal level of feeling that I never would have been at—a level that I wanted to be at but didn't know how to get there. I don't have the temper I used to have. . . . I've slowed down. . . . I was a very "Jack Rabbit" type of guy. I'd jump into anything. And it slowed me down to do some thinking. I think it's given me a better relationship with my kids, with my grandkids.

Clearly, almost all of the men reported highly positive experiences in the men's movement with the New Warriors. Indeed, a few of them even appeared to have idealized New Warrior leaders, at least initially. Adam disclosed that at first he tended to think that the leaders could do no wrong and that they would not possibly have any "ego problems." He explained that he "put them on a pedestal because I had experienced such intense love and nurturing and support." However, as he continued to work with them and as they shared their weaknesses with him, he gradually came "to see them in a more real way and down off their pedestals." Similarly, Ed initially idealized the leaders. "My initial impression was one of awe. Just wow! These guys are magic," he revealed. "They're special, super-human people. God, I really want to be like them." Eventually, though, Ed also realized that "they're just people—they don't walk on water." Somewhat disillusioned, Ed discovered that "they're not the great gurus I've envisioned them to be." He explained, "They've got a ton of shit that they're dragging behind them, just like me. And while some of their insights are good, some of them aren't so good." Harry also described the work of the leaders as "truly magical" and saluted "these brave and fearless men." However, after observing their "power trips," he, too, gradually relinquished his idealization of them and adopted a more realistic view.

While most of the men spoke very positively of the leadership of the men's movement, all of them nonetheless were able to articulate criticisms of the New Warriors. The most common criticism, registered by six of the men, was of the prohibitive cost of the weekend retreat and the Integration Group for the preliminary 2-month period (a sum of $600 in 1994), which they observed tended to exclude the less affluent. Barry, Harry, and Ian additionally complained about the bureaucracy, hierarchy, and "old-boy network" in the New Warrior organization. Ed and Greg expressed concern about amateurs in the New Warriors doing psychotherapy of sorts for which they are not trained and qualified. Perhaps in a related vein, Barry protested what he perceived to be "unfair attacks, confrontations, and orchestrations" that were made by some leaders during the weekend retreat. Frank criticized all of the "overanalyzing" of behavior, which he believed can be destructive to the men's love relationships. Adam stated that the New Warriors should be involved in more social and political campaigns, such as men's rights, fathers' rights, gender reconciliation, helping the homeless, saving the planet, and improving race relations and foreign relations. Ed criticized the New Warriors for focusing on the men's family-of-origin issues, for being "mired in the past," and for their arrogant use of jargon that outsiders do not understand. Lastly, Jim expressed sadness, frustration, and disappointment in New Warriors' lack of interest in carrying on friendships with him outside of the organization's activities. He commented, "I definitely went looking for community, and what I found often was merely an organization."

Despite such criticism, all of the men stated that they would recommend the New Warriors to other men, although some of them expressed reservations or made qualifications. Frank and Ian enthusiastically endorsed the New Warriors, stating that all men should go through the experience. Frank speculated that the world would be a safer place if all men experienced the New Warriors, as "we'd have less 'nut cases' going berserk because they'd have an outlet." Don said that he would recommend the New Warriors to most anyone, but he suggested that men with a college education and experience in psychotherapy would derive more benefits from it. Similarly, Greg claimed that he would recommend the New Warriors selectively to people with a capacity for insight. Ed expressed much ambivalence in addressing this question, as he found his experience with the New Warriors to be both beneficial and troubling, given the gains he made and his disagreement with the organization's alleged preoccupation with family-of-origin issues. Ed said that he would be inclined to say, "This is going to be the greatest thing in the world for you, but don't stay with it forever. Go through the weekend, go through six months of I-Group, and then get the fuck out of there."

At the time of their respective interviews, most of the men had regular contact with the New Warriors, although many of them were less involved with their Integration Groups than they had been in the past. Only Adam, Barry, and Greg appeared to be highly involved with their weekly support groups, with no imminent plans of withdrawing. Harry was meeting a couple of times a month with the remaining members of his shrunken Integration Group, and he seemed to be investing less than he had previously. Frank, who had been in an Integration Group for longer than any of the other men, for about 5 years, had pulled back in the last year because he had less of a need for it, as he had become more emotionally involved with his fiancé. Don also was withdrawing from his Integration Group because, he said, of diminishing returns, his general problem with commitment, the power of competing interests, and the inconvenience of traveling a long distance to the meeting place of his group. Ed had withdrawn and was definitely planning to leave because of the group's focus on the past. Carl had left his group because of his excessive involvement in therapy at that time in his life. Ian had left because he was satisfied with what he had received in his group and wanted no more. Lastly, Jim had left his group because of his aforementioned disappointment in trying to make friends, but he made the qualification that he consequently was not hostile to the men's movement and that he had not abandoned it.

Lastly, the men were asked if they and the other men who joined the men's movement or the New Warriors were different in some way—even before they joined—from other men who did not join. Adam replied, "The movement has tended to attract men who somehow have become aware of their own needs, their own lack of healthy relationships, their loneliness, their destructive tendencies with substance use." Barry replied, "I think the main thing is a crisis or some dissatisfaction with yourself that you want to deal with, that you are aware of. . ." Carl replied, "They were searching for answers that they hadn't found anywhere and were conscious of a need for some kind of higher power to get them to take a hard look at themselves." Don said that the men who seek out the New Warriors are "people on a path of self-actualization." Greg observed that the men who are drawn to the men's movement tend to be insightful men who "recognize there's a potential for a much more fulfilling life, and they don't know how to get there." Harry replied that all men have the capacity to seek out the New Warriors and that the decisive factor is "timing" in one's life. Ian suggested that men who join the New Warriors are either curious or discontented. Jim suggested that the men's movement attracts men who have a need for deep emotional contact with other men and who cannot satisfy that need through sports or conventional male friendship. Frank claimed that there was no difference between joiners and nonjoiners. The man who spoke most extensively about his view of the men who join the movement was Ed:

> The word that comes to my mind is "weakness." Either we're weak people in general, or we somehow were bestowed with the gift of being able to recognize weakness and do something about it. To me, most men out there are conditioned to saying that they have to be tough. There's a male role that they have to play.

And they wouldn't allow themselves to feel that fear and that weakness and go scouting for something like the Warriors. The men that do go seek out the Warriors are in trouble by and large. Why the fuck would they be going there if they weren't? Whatever their issue is, they've got a problem that they're trying to solve. And either they're very weak men, they have to do that, or they're perceptive men that seem to want to do this.

Chapter 8:
The Mythopoetic Men's Movement and Gender Politics

Feminists were generally hostile to the mythopoetic men's movement. Most feminist critics identified certain allegedly sexist aspects of the men's movement and tended to assume that the motivations of rank-and-file participants were congruent with them. Also, the critics recognized that the men's movement emerged in the 1980s, only a little more than a decade after the rise of the women's movement, during a period of antifeminist backlash, with a focus on the needs of men. Consequently, they tended to assume that the men's movement necessarily represented a hostile response to feminism. While both assumptions were reasonable, they might also have been false.

This chapter addresses the contentious question of whether or not, in what way, and to what degree the mythopoetic men's movement was sexist in the 1980s and early 1990s. The first part of this chapter is a presentation of the participants' perspectives on gender ideals and feminism. Such self-reports potentially provide insight into the motivations of participants and, thus, into their potential responses to women and feminism. Of course, the self-reports are limited by the participants' abilities to express themselves fully and honestly and by their awareness of their own motivations and latent potentials. Additionally, self-reports are no substitute for a critical analysis of such extra-individual factors as the movement's leadership, ideology, structure, practices, tendencies, possible future directions, and relationships to broader social forces and interests. Certainly, the men's movement whole is more than the mere sum of its individual constituents in any given moment. Therefore, in the second part of this chapter, these extra-individual factors, which were the target of feminist criticism, will be evaluated. Finally, in the third part of this chapter, the need for political change to solve the legitimate problems of men will be discussed.

Participants' Perspectives on Gender Ideals and Feminism

When the men were asked about their ideals about men, women, fathers, and mothers, they mostly gave answers that reflected support for basic, overall gender similarity and minimal gender differences. When they were asked what they thought a man should be and do and what they thought a woman should be and do, all of the men indicated that they believed that men and women should strive for the same non-gender-typed ideals. Typical of the responses was Harry's reply that both men and women should be honest, open, and sensitive. When asked what a father should be and do and then what a mother should be and do, the men similarly responded that both fathers and mothers should be highly emotionally involved with their children, spending quality time with them, nurturing them, guiding them, and teaching them. Four men—Adam, Barry, Don, and Jim—explicitly expressed support for the ideal of equal parenting. More traditional views were espoused by Ed, who believed that mainly the mother should provide the physical love, and by Frank, who believed that the father should be the main disciplinarian. However, even both of these men advocated similar roles for both parents overall. When asked about gender differences generally, the men tended to see more similarities than differences between men and women and to attribute any differences, such as women's greater emotional expressiveness, to culture, although some of them suggested that biology may be a factor as well.

When the men were asked what they thought about women working outside the home, they were generally supportive. Ian replied, "Fantastic! I don't think that should even be debatable." Similarly, Harry responded, "I think that it's great! The more the merrier!" Ed stated that the notion that a woman's place is at home is "nonsense," and he affirmed a woman's right "to pursue whatever career aspirations that she can have and to become whatever she can be." Jim declared, "I've never been able to understand how any man in the 20th century could object to that." Carl observed that women seeking paid employment is both important to their growth and economically necessary. Frank said that it was good, and he disclosed that he wants a "career woman" as a mate, although one who does not put her career over her family, as both men and women should put their families first. The remaining men each declared support for a woman's right to paid employment, but they also expressed concern about the prospect of children not receiving adequate attention, love, and supervision as a result of both parents working outside the home. Adam, Barry, and Don indicated that either parent could and should sacrifice work in order to insure that the children receive adequate care. Additionally, Adam asserted that one parent should remain home until the child reaches school age. Greg also indicated concern about the number of children being cared for by people outside the family.

When the men were asked about their opinions of the women's movement, they generally expressed support for its basic goal of gender equality. All of the men endorsed the principles of equal opportunity, equal pay for equal work, and the equal right of women to develop their full potential as human beings. Four of the men—Barry, Don, Greg, and Jim—indicated a close identification with feminist ideals. Harry simply praised the feminist movement as "wonderful" and affirmed, in a sincere, nonhostile way, women's right to "to fly jet fighters and go into combat." Carl observed that the feminist movement has helped women to "get ahead and get what they deserve." Although the men were not asked explicitly about their views on specific feminist demands, both Don and Harry volunteered that they supported a woman's right to abortion.

Within a basic framework of overall support of women's equality, most of the men also expressed some criticisms of feminists. Half of the men complained about the antimale rhetoric, generalized hostility to men, and other perceived excesses found in the women's movement. For example, Jim disagreed with those feminists who think that all or most men want to dominate women. Don suggested that mainstream feminists should celebrate women's differences more, and Carl criticized the women's movement for being too political and not concerned enough with personal growth and development. While very supportive overall, Adam expressed opposition to a key feminist demand, for child-care centers, because he believes that they are not good for the children. Although Ed acknowledged that the women's movement has "a lot of validity," he expressed strong opposition to feminist demands for legalized abortion, affirmative action, and a broad definition of sexual harassment. While he affirmed equal rights for women, Frank criticized feminists for attacking *Playboy* magazine as exploitative and for branding so many instances of men's sexual pursuit of women as sexual harassment. Out of all of the men, Frank expressed the most hostility to feminists when he angrily declared, "I can't stand feminists. . . . I think most of them end of up being lesbians, and there's a tremendous amount of hate built up for men that I've never been able to quite understand."

The men were informed that some feminists claimed that the men's movement represents part of a conservative backlash against the women's movement, and they were asked to address that charge. All of the men disputed the claim for the most part. Adam, Barry, and Jim conceded that some men and some men's groups, mainly in a different men's movement, might be hostile to women or aim to fight against women's rights. However, they asserted that such an antifeminist tendency is a tiny minority, not representative of the overriding thrust of the men's movement as a whole. Don strongly opposed the "backlash" charge: "It's not at all an antiwoman thing, not at all. It's a proman thing." Carl, Harry, and Ian all explained that feminists should not feel threatened by the men's movement, as it aims to help men "get in touch with their feelings" and still feel manly, not oppose women's rights. Greg declared that the men's movement did not represent a conservative backlash but, on the contrary, a liberal reaction to the feminist movement, insofar as it is trying to lead men out of their traditional role of oppressing women. Frank claimed that the notion that the men's movement is about women-bashing is a major misconception. He added that the men in his Integration Group generally express more anger toward other men—for example, their fathers and their bosses—than toward women.

Out of the 10 men, only Ed reported that he detected a hostile, blaming attitude toward women and a traditional, male chauvinistic stance among some men in the New Warriors—a position that he did not share. Ed observed that some of the men "take that 'Warrior' word very literally, that there's a superiority—this big masculine, macho thing, and that the woman belongs over here, down a few levels, you know, somewhat subservient." However, in contrast, Adam found that most of the men that he encountered in the men's movement tend to be generally more supportive of women's rights than most men, partly because of their involvement in the men's movement:

> My own experience has been that when men are involved in men's work they learn to respect women more, they learn to treat women better, they learn to have better relationships, that they are for women having equal rights. They are for sharing decision-making and homemaking and so on, or at least they tend to be more that way than many of the men I've known who haven't been involved.

Although Ian asserted that the men's movement does not constitute a conservative backlash against the women's movement, he stated that he believes that contemporary feminism nonetheless precipitated a crisis of male identity that contributed to the rise of the men's movement. He elaborated, somewhat metaphorically, on the source of contemporary men's insecurity:

> The assault by women, who are asking for what they rightfully deserve and challenging a lot of men's traditional feelings. And, you know. . . no longer in the marriage vows they say "love, honor, and obey." And the "obey" part is fucking gone now, and that threatens a lot of men and questions their authority. I think that sometimes men feel like a ship without a rudder and insecure as a result of all the things that are required of them today.

Feminist Analysis and Assessment

This section offers a feminist analysis and assessment of the mythopoetic men's movement, including an assessment of the criticisms that feminists made of the movement through the mid-1990s. Although the movement featured certain implicitly conservative elements regarding gender, it did not explicitly oppose the struggle for women's equality. Certainly, the movement did not promote an antifeminist political agenda (or any overt political agenda for that matter). The movement did not organize or campaign against legalized abortion, antidiscrimination legislation, affirmative action, comparable worth (pay equity), paid parental leave, child-care facilities, etc. While women's increasing employment and the feminist movement surely helped to precipitate the contemporary crisis of male identity that gave rise to the men's movement, the leaders of the men's movement did not speak out against women's employment or the central feminist goal of women's full social, economic, and political equality with men.

However, in their main writings, leaders of the men's movement did make two substantial criticisms of feminism. One criticism was that feminists instigate male-bashing. Bly (1990) suggested that feminist attacks on patriarchy led mothers to discount grown men to their sons and inspired wives and girlfriends to criticize their mates as chauvinistic. Moore and Gillette (1990) identified "an outright demonization of men and a slander against masculinity" perpetrated by feminists (p. 156). Similarly, Kipnis (1991) charged feminists with encouraging powerful antimale trends in popular culture.

The leaders of the men's movement rightly opposed male-bashing, but only where male-bashing refers to the categorical vilification and denunciation of men. Here, male-bashing is distinguished from legitimate feminist criticism of male privilege and male sexism, although there is admittedly a gray area where the two blend into each other. Flowing from women's understandable anger at men for male domination, abuse, and irresponsibility, male-bashing was not a fair or constructive response to these problems. However, just as legitimate feminist criticism sometimes turned into male-bashing, opposition to male-bashing sometimes turned into a defensive rejection of legitimate feminist criticism. Many men rejected feminist criticism not necessarily because they were invested in male privilege and male sexist behavior, but because they took such criticism personally, that is, they felt psychologically threatened by perceived attacks on the male sex, of which they were members and with which they were deeply identified. Thus, Bly seemed to dismiss the possibility that in any given instance wives and girlfriends might be justified in criticizing their mates as chauvinistic. Instead, Bly wrongly implied that any time a woman called a man chauvinistic she was engaging in male-bashing.

The second main criticism that the men's movement made of feminism was Bly's (1990) claim that the feminist movement had contributed to the widespread development of a softness, including an enervation and passivity, in contemporary American men. As previously mentioned in the discussion of *Iron John*, Bly seemed to have based this claim of passivity in men on his observations of the young men that he had encountered in the milieu of poets, feminist spiritualists, and commune-dwellers—a decidedly unusual sample of men, who would hardly be representative of American men as a whole. Although a tiny minority of misguided men may have overreacted to the feminist critique of male domination by giving up all assertiveness, much as Bly suggested, the reason for such self-renunciation would probably lie with these men's misplaced sense of guilt and loss of perspective in response to feminism, not with some debilitating power of feminism in and of itself.

The solution that Bly (1990) proposed to the alleged problem of passivity in men is that men develop their "deep masculinity" and "fierceness." Bly implicitly defined these traits as decisiveness and resolve and explicitly distinguished them from savagery and cruelty. While some readers may confuse "fierceness" with traditional male aggression because of the usual meaning of this word, the quality that Bly seemed to be advocating is a passionate assertion of the self that nonetheless respects the needs and rights of others. Still, the criticism of softness, combined with the promotion of "fierceness," can unfortunately mislead men into rejecting sensitivity and other positive qualities that have traditionally been designated by the culture as feminine. Such a development would conflict with the movement's general thrust of facilitating, through its group processes, men's capacity for empathy, intimacy, and mutual emotional support.

Bly (1990) argued that boys must develop their so-called deep masculinity by breaking from their mothers. Although Bly implicitly endorsed the assignment of the role of "civilizing" boys to their mothers, he also criticized mothers as extremely possessive. Bly therefore advocated fathers' greater involvement in rearing their sons, especially when they are older. However, his implication that mothers should be the primary caregivers, from whom sons must subsequently break, might discourage fathers from sharing child care equally, especially when the children are younger. Moreover, as previously mentioned in the discussion of *Iron John*, empirical research findings suggested that a warm relationship with the father—not a break from the mother—facilitates the development of a satisfactory psychosocial adjustment in boys (Lamb, 1986). While there certainly are mothers who are overinvolved with and possessive of their children in this culture which idealizes women's capacity for nurturance and devalues their other capacities, Bly overgeneralized from such mothers and thereby encouraged undue separation and differentiation of sons from their mothers.

Leaders of the men's movement also argued that males must develop their "deep" or "mature" masculinity by being initiated into the community of men (Bly, 1990; Moore & Gillette, 1990). Although the men's movement primarily provided male-initiation-like experiences to grown men, leaders vaguely advocated the establishment of some form of male initiation of boys to help them develop secure male identities. Certainly, the institutionalized male-initiation practices of other cultures have marked and facilitated the transition of adolescent males from boyhood to manhood. However, these practices have derived their psychological meaning and power from the surrounding society's clearly defined and agreed-upon gender roles, relations, and expectations. The implantation of male-initiation practices in contemporary Western society is not likely to help boys develop secure gender identities so long as the meaning of manhood remains unclear and contentious in the broader culture. Furthermore, aside from the issue of its viability, the establishment of formal male-initiation practices in Western society would be completely unjustified to the extent that, like in other cultures, they also promoted male domination or sexist limitations on the full human potential of either males or females.

Some feminists asserted that even the men's movement's existing practice of excluding women from its gatherings was unjustified. Indeed, feminists likened this exclusion of women to whites' exclusion of blacks from events that are open to the public (Johnston, 1992; Ruether, 1992). The problem with this analogy, however, was that it obscured important differences between gender relations and race relations and between the purposes and consequences of exclusion in these two cases. Both race relations and gender relations are based partly on power and oppression, i.e., white domination and male domination, respectively. However, the relations between women and men, unlike the relations between blacks and whites, also consist largely of intimate bonds and interpersonal obligations that meet, albeit through rigid and dichotomous roles, most men and women's legitimate needs for love, sex, material support, and the reproduction and rearing of the next generation. Reflecting the centrality of these bonds and the polarity of these roles, gender socialization is more deeply defining, differentiating, and restricting of individuals than racial socialization, which, in contrast, is not at all aimed at preparing individuals for dichotomous role-playing in intimate relations with members of other races. Thus, when whites exclude blacks, they usually do so because of racism, not because they need to meet separately in order to solve some kind of specifically white problem imposed on them by racial socialization. However, when men exclude women, they usually do so either because of sexism *or* because they need to meet separately to address the legitimate issues and concerns of men as men, including problems related to their socialization into an emotionally constricting (though materially privileging) gender role.

It does not appear that the all-male gatherings of the men's movement were aimed at, or had the consequences of, promoting male domination. As suggested by the men interviewed for this study, the function of the all-male character of the gatherings was to facilitate men's self-disclosure and bonding in the course of personal growth, development, and psychological healing. Unlike other discriminatory practices, such as discrimination against women in education and employment, the movement practice of limiting the gatherings to men did not exclude women from powerful or prestigious positions or deprive them of resources that affect the quality of their lives. While such all-male space did give men the opportunity and the permission to express anger toward women (*and* men) in their lives, it does not follow that this anger would translate into an antifeminist or otherwise antagonistic attitude toward women. However, the absence of women from the gatherings did deprive the men of women's perspectives and increased the probability that any sexist comments would go unchallenged. (This potential problem is not unique to the men's movement but is common to male interactions generally.) Also, the example that the movement set of excluding women might inspire other groups and organizations to enact, in the name of "respecting" gender differences, forms of gender segregation that, intentionally or unintentionally, perpetuate gender inequality or impose sexist limitations on either males or females.

Perhaps the most serious problem with the men's movement, from a feminist perspective, was its biological essentialism. Although Bly (1990) did not explicitly claim that women do not also possess a capacity for decisiveness and resolve, his designation of these qualities as "deep masculinity" wrongly implied that they are innately and exclusively male traits. Similarly, although Moore and Gillette (1990) did not explicitly claim that women do not also possess a capacity for leadership, their attribution of this trait to a genetically transmitted male archetype (the King archetype) wrongly implied that it is natural to men only. These writings, along with other Jungian-informed analysis of gender in the movement, inadvertently though readily lent themselves to a justification of different and unequal social roles for women and men. This tendency was further facilitated by the movement's use of warrior imagery and fairy tales, which contain stereotypical, male-dominant notions of gender roles and relations.

Feminists argued that men, as members of the dominant sex, have a moral responsibility to fight for women's liberation, and they therefore criticized the men's movement for failing to adopt an explicitly feminist mission. Kimmel and Kaufman (1994) asserted that participants in the men's movement "would rather complain about something they can barely change," that is, their painful childhood experiences with their estranged fathers, "than work toward transforming something that they can: their relationships with their own children and structural inequalities of power between men and women, adults and children, and one man and another" (p. 282). Considering the self-reports of the New Warriors presented here, Kimmel and Kaufman were mistaken in suggesting that men's movement participants were not interested in improving their relationships with their children, but these feminist critics were basically correct in claiming that the men as a group are not interested in eradicating social inequality. However, only a tiny progressive-minded percentage of the general public—female as well as male—appeared to be interested in participating in political struggles to combat social inequality in the 1990s. Moreover, only a tiny minority of women have ever participated in the struggle for women's equality specifically, despite the direct, collective self-interest of women to do so. Given the extent of men's gender-based privileges and socialization and given participants' focus on their own personal issues, it was even less likely that the men's movement could be directed to fight for the worthy goal of women's liberation, as many feminists moralistically demanded.

Conservative forces in the men's movement conceivably could tap the implicitly conservative elements in the movement to steer it, or at least a sector of it, into right-wing politics, as feared by feminist critics (Clatterbaugh, 1993; Kimmel, 1996b). The men's movement could come to support explicitly antifeminist campaigns, such as those against abortion rights and affirmative action, or the electoral campaigns of conservative politicians. Alternatively, the men's movement might become more closely allied with the fathers' rights movement, which lobbies for legislative changes in child custody, child support awards, and abortion, to increase men's power in these areas. Another possibility is that it would associate with the Promise Keepers, a religious men's movement that draws men to all-male gatherings in sports arenas for prayer, repentance, male bonding, and commitment to conservative Christian values. Such developments might be facilitated by a possible latent tendency among participants to preserve the gender-based privileges of men, by the participants' search for solutions to the contemporary crisis of male identity, and by the movement's lack of an explicitly feminist orientation. These developments would be more likely to occur in the context of a rise of a popular mass antifeminist movement in the larger society.

The relative importance and weight of the implicitly conservative elements in the men's movement should not be exaggerated, however. Considering the self-reports of the New Warriors presented here and the investigator's own personal observations while participating in the weekend retreat and support group, the men's movement does not seem to have attracted generally antifeminist men or to have influenced participants to move in an antifeminist direction. A narrow focus on the implicitly conservative elements in the movement literature can obscure the more substantive, relevant, and positive nonconservative elements that predominate and that appear to be the main reasons for the participants' involvement, namely, such activities as introspection and mutual emotional support. If the men in this study are representative of men in the men's movement, it can safely be assumed that most of the men in the movement are concerned with exploring their inner lives, working on their interpersonal relationships, bonding with other men, and healing their psychological wounds, not with renegotiating power with women, either to the advantage or disadvantage of women.

The right-wing political potential of the men's movement should not be overestimated either. Feminist critics seemed to exaggerate the inclination and potential toward political action on the part of the participants in the men's movement. Men seeking personal growth and development will not easily be moved to engage in controversial political activism, with all of its attendant tension, conflict, and focus beyond the needs of the individual self. Consequently, the men's movement is more likely to remain mostly apolitical, especially in the current, relatively quiescent political period. Thus, on the whole, despite its implicitly conservative elements, the men's movement in its present form does not constitute a threat to the struggle for women's equality. Nonetheless, the men's movement should discard and disavow its conservative elements in order to diminish its antifeminist potential and help prevent conservative forces from steering the movement into right-wing politics.

The Need for Progressive Change

The basically apolitical orientation of the mythopoetic men's movement is both its main strength and its main weakness. This assessment holds true at least from the point of view of solving the legitimate problems of men, such as fathers' relative underinvolvement in child rearing and men's relative lack of emotional intimacy in interpersonal relationships, especially with each other. The movement's lack of a political perspective potentially encourages men of all political beliefs to come together to address their personal problems and meet their needs for social support, male validation, personal growth and development, and psychotherapeutic healing. Such an opportunity is very beneficial to individual participants and is therefore worth defending. If the men's movement were to adopt an explicit and controversial political agenda, especially a progressive agenda in the current conservative political climate, it would likely alienate much of its potential constituency, create discord among its ranks, lead many to withdraw, precipitate a split in the movement, and ultimately destroy the movement. Therefore, the men's movement must remain a primarily personal-development movement and not adopt a controversial political orientation in order to sustain itself, maximize its appeal, and continue to heal the wounds of individual men.

However, while the benefits of the men's movement can be significant for individual participants, they are likely to remain extremely limited for men as a whole, even if the movement were able to disseminate its ideas widely throughout society, beyond movement gatherings. Although an apolitical personal-development movement possesses the potential to heal the existing wounds of men who seek it out, it does not possess sufficient power to prevent the ongoing infliction of such wounds on the masses of men in the first place. The foregoing psychosocial analysis suggests that efforts must be made that go beyond narrow individual intervention at the intrapsychic and interpersonal levels. Therefore, forces other than the men's movement must make political changes at the broader societal and institutional levels to attack the social roots of men's legitimate problems.

The collective solutions to men's legitimate problems lie with progressive social change. Men must challenge the existing gender-based division of labor and power and the existing class-based division of labor and power, including the current distribution of wealth, if they want to help solve men's legitimate problems as a sex. Paradoxically, this entails confronting men's historic privileges over women, as well as the historic power that the most economically privileged men exercise over other men and women alike.

Only comprehensive progressive change can attack the social roots of men's legitimate problems without undermining women's struggle for equality in the process.

Indeed, part of the solution to men's relative overinvolvement in breadwinning and their corresponding underinvolvement in child rearing lies with the implementation of a feminist political agenda. Women gaining equality in paid employment would alleviate the disproportionate financial burden on their husbands or mates to support their families. Women can achieve equality in the work force with the help of a strong enforcement of existing antidiscrimination legislation, the expansion of affirmative action, and the institution of comparable worth (pay equity). Also, the establishment of flexible working hours, paid parental leave, and low-cost, high-quality child-care facilities, as well as defense of safe, legal and accessible abortion, would provide women with alternatives to sacrificing work for the sake of their children and because of unwanted pregnancies, respectively. Additionally, men and their relationships with their children would benefit directly from flexible working hours and paid parental leave.

With these feminist reforms, some of the financial gains that men would make as husbands or mates of well-paid women workers would be cancelled out by the losses that they would sustain as competitors of highly competitive women workers in the job market. However, these losses could be more than offset for most working-class and middle-class men by other far-reaching leftist economic reforms. The unionizing of the work force, including workers in the service and white-collar sectors of the economy, could help both male and female employees make gains in pay through collective bargaining and thereby increase their financial ability to devote less time to work and more time to their families. Also, a massive government-funded public works program, financed by cutting the military budget and imposing a highly progressive income tax on the wealthy, could provide jobs and job training at union wages and with union benefits to anyone who wants to work. Such a public works program would be aimed at building public schools, hospitals, health clinics, child-care centers, recreation centers, etc.; expanding mass transit and safe, renewable energy sources; and repairing the nation's deteriorating infrastructure, including its roads, bridges, and water systems. Additionally, a program of government-funded child support allowances and/or tax credits to parents could help ease the financial burden of raising children.

Ultimately, the most effective solution to the problem of men's overinvolvement in breadwinning and underinvolvement in child rearing lies with a drastic reduction of the hours in the work week with no cut in weekly pay. Such a measure would enable parents to devote more time to their children without sacrificing their incomes and material standard of living in the process. Provided that overtime is eliminated, the reduction in the work week would additionally create new jobs. Despite the enormous growth in national productivity since the Second World War, the work week has not been reduced in the United States since Congress passed the Fair Labor Act in 1938, making the 8-hour day and the 40-hour week the law of the land (Roediger & Foner, 1989). As early as the late 1940s, though, two major labor unions—the United Autoworkers and the United Steelworkers—resolved in favor of 30 hours of work for 40 hours of pay.

While such sweeping reforms are necessary to provide men with the increased time and financial ability to become more involved with their children, these reforms are not sufficient to produce this desired outcome. Men must be given not only the opportunity but the motivation to devote themselves more to child rearing. Thus, additional reforms that tap into socialization, identification, and internalization processes must be implemented. Such reforms could include educational campaigns in the media and the schools that explicitly advocate fathers' greater participation in child care and that teach males both the emotional and physical aspects of routine child care. Also, the active recruitment of men to positions as teachers, especially at the preschool and grade school levels, and as workers in child-care centers would provide boys with male role models with whom they could identify and thereby internalize new expectations for nurturance in males. (Initially, both the low pay and prestige accorded to these female-dominated occupations would probably have to be upgraded significantly in order to attract men to these fields, which have historically been devalued, along with child care generally, in a society dominated by the market.) Eventually, males would observe that nurturance and child care are not feminine activities that threaten their masculine identities or invite social disapproval or rejection by other males.

The problems of men's relationships could also be solved through such progressive social change. The aforementioned reforms that increase men's ability to work less hours would free up men for more time with friends as well as family. With new opportunities for friendship and extra-familial ties, men could challenge the unrealistic notion that the private nuclear family and the companionate marriage could and should meet all of their needs for social support. The increase in job security and the new importance placed on social life outside of work could reduce the pressures on men to compete for jobs, wealth, prestige, and status in the market, one of the chief causes of the alienation of men from each other in industrial capitalist society. Changes in male socialization practices, partly aided by the aforementioned reforms in education and child care, could instill new expectations in males to be interpersonally sensitive and emotionally intimate in close relationships, including with other males. Additionally, progress that gays make in winning equal rights and general support and acceptance in society would diminish homophobia, an important impediment to men's ability to be emotionally intimate with each other. The consequent diminution of gender differences created by such reforms would greatly reduce the importance of gender as an organizing principle in matters outside of sex and reproduction. Indeed, the ultimate, progressive solution to the male insecurity registered by the mythopoetic men's movement is the elimination of gender polarization.

The combination of feminist and leftist reforms proposed here as solutions to the legitimate problems of men entail radical challenges to both men's historic privileges over women and the historic power that the capitalist class exercises over the working class and middle class. Thus, the demand for such sweeping changes is sure to be met with strong resistance from antifeminists, big business and its supporters, and other defenders of the status quo. Such resistance is likely to be overcome only through the countervailing power of popular and militant mass movements—mainly a revitalized feminist movement and a revitalized labor movement. Only the masses of women, mobilized in the streets behind feminist demands, possess sufficient self-interest and the ability to lead the struggle for women's equality. Only the working class, organized in its unions and mobilized at the workplace and in the streets, has both the necessary economic self-interest and power, given its strategic concentration at the point of production and its corresponding potential to shut down production, to force the government to institute broad leftist economic reforms—or to replace the corporate-dominated government if necessary with one that would institute such reforms. In the

United States, the labor movement successfully led the struggle for such progressive legislation as the right to strike, the right to bargain collectively, the 8-hour day, the minimum wage, unemployment insurance, and Social Security (Piven & Cloward, 1977). In other advanced capitalist nations, such as in Western Europe, the much stronger labor movements there and their affiliated political parties—including the Labour, Social Democratic, Socialist, and Communist parties—have won even greater gains for their working-class constituencies. These greater gains include a shorter work week, universal health insurance, universal paid vacation, more child-care facilities and paid parental leave, and more extensive social services generally (Stephens, 1986).

Thus, the collective solutions to the legitimate problems of men, if they are to be provided, will not be provided by the mythopoetic men's movement. The men who constitute the men's movement are primarily motivated by a search for individual and therapeutic solutions, not collective solutions, to their personal problems. Moreover, most of the constituents of the men's movement are white middle-class men. While most middle-class men would benefit both psychologically and materially from progressive social change overall, on the whole they probably would not play a leading role in challenging the established economic and political order. Middle-class men as a group enjoy too many relative material privileges, are too atomized within the economy, and have too close working relationships with and ties to the rich and the powerful to play such a leading role. This is not to say that individual middle-class men or sectors of middle-class men, including men in the men's movement, could not be won over to a progressive political perspective, especially in the context of a revitalization of the labor movement and/or the feminist movement. Indeed, in the event of such a hypothetical development, many men in the men's movement probably would move leftward and support such progressive change, given their already heightened awareness of gender issues.

In the absence of major political developments in the larger society, however, the men's movement itself is likely to remain mostly apolitical. After all, the movement essentially represents a mass therapeutic response to the contemporary crisis of male identity and to the problems of traditional male experience. As such, it simply aims to heal the wounds of masculinity—both the wounds inflicted *on* traditional masculinity *and* the wounds inflicted *by* traditional masculinity. In so doing, it reaffirms such positive traits as strength and assertiveness, which this gender-polarizing culture has designated as masculine. At the same time, it helps men develop those positive aspects of their personalities, such as sensitivity and nurturance, which the culture has designated as feminine and therefore stigmatized in men. Partly adapting to the gender-polarizing culture, the men's movement has attempted to redefine these traditionally feminine characteristics as masculine, rather than simply as *human*. Paradoxically, it also has moved men to separate from women, in support groups and on weekend retreats, in personal quests to become, in effect, more like women in certain positive respects. Perhaps the power and tenacity of gender identity require men, at least some men, to take a proverbial step back before taking two steps forward.

Chapter 9:
Summary

In January 1990, the American public was introduced to the mythopoetic men's movement with the broadcast of *A Gathering of Men* on public television. Started by the distinguished poet Robert Bly in the early 1980s, the men's movement is primarily a personal-development movement that aims to rebuild and revitalize male community and heal the psychological wounds of men, primarily through ritual male bonding. Although it received much public attention in the early 1990s, few psychologists or other social scientists have researched the men's movement, despite its obvious relevance to the related fields of psychology and psychotherapy. The purpose of this study is to offer a psychosocial analysis of the rise of the men's movement. Written from a social constructionist perspective, this analysis draws mainly on the psychological, sociological, and historical literature on and relevant to American men. It also is based on interviews, conducted in 1994, of 10 fairly representative participants in the Chicago branch of the New Warriors (since renamed the ManKind Project), a men's movement organization. Additionally, the analysis draws on the writer's own limited personal involvement in the men's movement as both an observer and participant, also in 1994.

The Psychosocial Analysis

The central thesis of this analysis is that the mythopoetic men's movement represents a mass therapeutic response primarily to a crisis of male identity that men, especially middle-class men, have widely experienced in varying degrees in the United States since the 1970s. This crisis of male identity consists mainly of the collective experience of loss produced by challenges to traditional masculinity, particularly its central feature, the male breadwinner ethic. This ethic became the central feature of traditional masculinity in the 19th century, in the wake of the Industrial Revolution, which split work life and family life into two separate public and private spheres, respectively, and which relegated men to the public sphere of paid employment. After the Second World War, five main social developments challenged the male breadwinner ethic: the search of self-fulfillment, women's increasing employment, the sexual revolution, the feminist movement, and, since the 1970s, the economic crisis. Beginning in the 1970s, the escalation and convergence of these five main challenges, compounded by the consequent decline of male commitment and the corresponding appearance of male-bashing, produced a crisis of male identity.

    The contemporary crisis of male identity enabled and motivated many men to reflect critically upon and reevaluate certain features of traditional male experience, including fathers' relative underinvolvement in child rearing. This particular feature of traditional male experience was especially problematic because it interfered with boys' largely socially constructed need to bond with their fathers in order to help them masculinize themselves in a culture that maintains and values a high level of differentiation between males and females. The origins of the alienation of fathers from sons lie with social developments in industrial society. These developments included the relegation of fathers to paid employment outside the home, the displacement of the father by the mother as the primary parent, the transfer of certain socialization functions from the family to the state and the professions, the strengthening of the adolescent peer group and the rise of the youth subculture, the devaluation of the older generations by mass culture, and the increase in women's relative influence in the family after the Second World War. The consequences of paternal underinvolvement for sons are that they feel grief for their lack of close relationships with their fathers and that they are put at risk for problems in the areas of achievement orientation, psychosocial adjustment, and gender role conformity, which is a potential source of anxiety, shame, and diminished self-esteem in a gender-polarizing culture.

    The crisis of male identity also enabled and motivated men to reevaluate another feature of traditional male experience, namely, men's relative lack of emotional intimacy in interpersonal relationships, especially with each other. This feature is problematic because it impairs men's ability to meet their innate human need for general social support and their largely socially constructed masculine need for male validation. The origins of the alienation of men from other men lie with social developments in industrial society. In the 19th century, these developments included the breakdown of traditional communities caused by urbanization, the promotion of competition by free market forces and capitalist ideology, and the corresponding socialization of male to be emotionally tough and constricted. In the 20th century, these developments included the intensification of heterosexual relationships with women, the elevation of private family life, the spread of an increased abhorrence of homosexuality, and the growing desegregation of men and women. Partly as a consequence of some of these developments, contemporary male relationships lack direct intimacy—the sharing of vulnerable thoughts and feelings. This deficit predisposes men to psychosomatic problems, aggressive behavior, alcohol and drug abuse, decreased sensitivity to their own and others' feelings, and a lack of adequate emotional support in the face of problems.

Robert Bly and other leaders of the mythopoetic men's movement responded to the crisis of male identity, the problems of father-son relationships, and the problems of men's relationships by functioning as charismatic leaders to help men cope with these problems. The leadership functioned in this way partly by offering an explanation of men's problems. Much of this explanation can be found in Bly's book *Iron John*, which essentially states that men have been wounded insofar as they have been deprived of close relationships with their fathers and of institutionalized initiation into the male community. The appeal of *Iron John* to male readers lies with its various elements, including Bly's responsiveness to the wounds of men, the simplicity of his reliance on fairy tales, his support for popular notions of essential gender differences, and his support for sons' definitive separation from their mothers. Influenced by both traditional and contemporary expectations of men, male readers probably also appreciate Bly's rejection of both machismo and feminine-like passivity in men, along with his support for determination, resolve, sensitivity, and nurturance in men.

The leaders of the men's movement also offered a solution to the problems of men by drawing on the existing therapeutic culture to give men a form of mass psychotherapy to heal their psychological wounds. This therapeutic culture was fashioned in the 20th century out of the rise in general affluence, the social breakdown of community and tradition, and shifts in the economy that fostered the kind of mental and interpersonal skills and characteristics that are conducive to psychotherapy. Like most psychotherapy since the 1960s, the men's movement partly aimed, in its support groups and weekend retreats, to help men develop those parts of their personalities that the culture traditionally has designated as feminine and has stigmatized in men, e.g., their capacity for self-disclosure and emotional support. It also promotes such substantial traditional masculine elements as strength, assertiveness, and male bonding. Additionally, it features certain stylistic masculine elements, such as drumming and the image of the warrior, probably partly to provide psychological compensation for men engaging in such stigmatized feminine activities as sharing intimate feelings and crying.

The Interviews of the Participants

The material from the interviews of the 10 participants in the New Warriors is generally supportive of, or at least compatible with, this foregoing psychosocial analysis. Demographically, most of the men were white, middle class, middle-aged, and heterosexual. Most of them reported unsatisfactory, if not extremely negative, relationships with their fathers that reflect the general alienation of fathers from sons in industrial American society. They all reported that their fathers generally were not demonstrative or expressive of affection, and some reported experiences of mental and/or physical abuse. A majority of the men expressed serious grievances against their mothers, for a variety of reasons. Half of the men reported problematic relations with male peers while growing up, as predicted by the research findings on boys lacking positive relationships with fathers. Reflecting the social significance of gender role conformity, the five men who did not have such problems as boys all reported a high interest and involvement in sports, around which most young male friendships center. When asked to state what they thought are the main problems of men, all of the participants identified problems related to the socialization of males to be emotionally tough and to refrain from expressing their feelings of vulnerability.

All 10 men had been involved in psychotherapy or some form of mental health treatment before becoming involved in the men's movement. Indeed, five of them were referred to the New Warriors by therapists that they were seeing at the time. Most of the men reported that they became involved in the New Warriors in response to a serious problem or crisis in their lives, such as a drug addiction, a divorce, severe depression, or significant interpersonal difficulties. Most of the men identified such problems, combined with a willingness to get help or an interest in personal growth, as the main characteristics that distinguished them from most other men who do not become involved in the men's movement. They generally claimed that what they and other participants valued about the New Warriors was the emotional support and male bonding that the gatherings provide. Almost all of the men reported significant, positive changes in their lives as a result of their involvement. Although they generally claimed that they would recommend the New Warriors to other men, they also were critical of the organization for a variety of reasons. The most common complaint was the prohibitive cost of the weekend retreat and follow-up Integration Group for the preliminary 2-month period (a sum total of $600 in 1994).

When asked about their views on various gender issues, few of the men expressed ideas or sentiments that could be interpreted as antifeminist or misogynist. While most of the men supported the all-male character of men's movement groups and retreats, their position seemed to flow from two notions: (1) the belief that women's presence would inhibit men's ability to freely express their thoughts and feelings, for reasons largely related to their different gender-based experiences, and (2) the belief that men have a special need for specifically male recognition, validation, and bonding. When asked about their ideals about men, women, fathers, and mothers, they mostly gave answers that reflected support for basic, overall gender similarity and minimal gender differences. When the men were asked about what they thought about women working outside the home, they were generally supportive. When they were asked about their opinions of the women's movement, they generally expressed support for its basic goal of gender equality, although they also expressed some criticisms of feminists, especially for the anti-male rhetoric, generalized hostility toward men, and other perceived excesses found in the women's movement. For the most part, all of the men disputed the claim made by feminists that the men's movement represents part of a conservative backlash against the women's movement.

The Political Conclusions

Despite the general lack of opposition to women's equality among the New Warriors presented here, the mythopoetic men's movement featured certain implicitly conservative elements and incipient tendencies toward antifeminism, particularly in the writings of key leaders. These elements include a tendency to deflect legitimate feminist criticism by confusing it with male-bashing, a tendency to blame feminism for an alleged development of passivity in contemporary men, and an unintended potential to discourage sensitivity in males (even as a stronger, countervailing tendency facilitates sensitivity in males). The men's movement also might encourage undue separation of sons from mothers, while it implicitly, uncritically accepts the dominant norm that women should be the primary caregivers of children (even as it encourages fathers' greater involvement in child rearing overall). The main drawbacks of the all-male character of the movement gatherings are that it deprives men of women's perspectives and that it might inspire other groups to enact retrograde forms of gender segregation. Perhaps the most serious problem with the men's movement, from a feminist perspective, is its postulation of a biological essentialist conception of gender, which inadvertently lends itself to a justification of different and unequal roles for women and men. This problem is reinforced by the movement's use of warrior imagery and fairy tales, which contain stereotypical, male-dominant notions of gender roles and relations.

Conservative forces in the men's movement conceivably could tap these implicitly conservative elements to steer the movement, or at least a sector of it, into right-wing politics. However, neither the relative weight of these conservative elements nor the right-wing political potential of the men's movement should be overestimated. The men's movement does not seem to have attracted generally antifeminist men, does not seem to have moved them in an antifeminist direction, and is not likely to engage them in controversial political activism, given the men's focus on personal growth and development. Consequently, the men's movement is more likely to remain mostly apolitical and not pose a threat to the struggle for women's equality. Nonetheless, the movement should discard and disavow its conservative elements in order to diminish its antifeminist potential.

In order to sustain itself and attract the largest number of men who could potentially benefit from it, the men's movement must remain a primarily personal-development movement and not adopt a controversial political orientation. However, an apolitical personal-development movement does not possess sufficient power to attack the social roots of the legitimate problems of men, which can only be solved through progressive political change. Feminist reforms that would help women to gain equality in paid employment would simultaneously alleviate the disproportionate financial burden on their husbands and mates to support their families and would thereby free them up for more time with their children. Such reforms include the strong enforcement of antidiscrimination legislation, the expansion of affirmative action, the institution of comparable worth (pay equity), flexible working hours, paid parental leave, and child-care facilities, and the defense of safe, legal, and accessible abortion. Other, leftist economic reforms that would enable both working-class and middle-class parents to devote more time to their children without sacrificing their incomes include increased unionization, a massive public works program, government-funded child support allowances and/or increased tax credits to parents, and a reduction of the hours in the work week with no cut in weekly pay. Additional reforms that tap into socialization, identification and internalization processes, such as educational campaigns and the active recruitment of men to positions as teachers and child-care workers, would increase the motivation of men to devote themselves more to child rearing. All of these reforms, combined with changes in male socialization practices generally and the struggle against homophobia, would also help to solve the problem of the relative lack of emotional intimacy in men's interpersonal relationships.

Such reforms are likely to be won only by revitalized, militant mass feminist and labor movements. Only women possess sufficient self-interest and the ability to lead the struggle for feminist reforms. Only the organized working class has both the necessary economic self-interest and power to bring about broad leftist economic reforms. While middle-class men, including men in the men's movement, can be won to such progressive social change, they do not possess either sufficient self-interest or the power to lead the struggle for such change. Moreover, the participants in the men's movement are primarily motivated by a search for individual and therapeutic solutions, not collective solutions, to their personal problems.

The future of the mythopoetic men's movement is unclear at this point. The public attention that it received in the early 1990s has decreased dramatically. However, twenty years later, the website of the ManKind Project (formerly the New Warriors) could boast that it was active in more than 40 communities in the United States and seven other countries and that more than 50,000 men had completed the New Warrior Training Adventure weekend retreat. Whatever becomes of the movement, the important gender issues of men that it has raised are not likely to fade away, short of major social, economic and political change. The progressive struggle to solve the legitimate problems of men as a sex will require much hard work, determination, and a willingness to fight—all elements of traditional masculinity. To borrow the mythopoetic, gender-polarizing words of Robert Bly (1990), that struggle will require Wild Man energy, which "leads to forceful action undertaken, not with cruelty, but with resolve" (p. 8).

References

Adams, P. L., Milner, J. R., & Schrepf, N. A. (1984). *Fatherless children*. New York: John Wiley.

Adler, J. (1991, June 24). Drums, sweat and tears. *Newsweek*, pp. 46-53.

Alexie, S. (1992, October 4). White men can't drum. *The New York Times Magazine*, pp. 30-31.

Allen, M. (1993). *In the company of men: A new approach to healing for husbands, fathers, and friends*. New York: Random House.

Astrachan, A. (1986). *How men feel: Their responses to women's demands for equality and power*. Garden City, New York: Anchor Press/Doubleday.

Back, K. W. (1987). *Beyond words: The story of sensitivity training and the encounter movement* (2nd ed.). New Brunswick, New Jersey: Transaction Books.

Bader, M. J., & Philipson, I. J. (1980). Narcissism and family structure. *Psychoanalysis and Contemporary Thought, 3*(3), 299-328.

Baldauf, G. (1993, October). Keynote address at Men's Day conference at Oakton Community College, DesPlaines, Illinois.

Balswick, J. (1988). *The inexpressive male*. Lexington, Massachusetts: Lexington Books.

Bardwick, J. (1979). *In transition: How feminism, sexual liberation, and the search for self-fulfillment have altered our lives*. New York: Holt, Rinehart & Winston.

Barton, E. R. (2000). Preface. In E. R. Barton (Ed.), *Mythopoetic perspectives of men's healing work: An anthology for therapists and others* (pp. xi-xiii). Westport, Connecticut: Bergin & Garvey.

Basow, S. A. (1992). *Gender: Stereotypes and roles* (3rd ed.). Pacific Grove, California: Brooks/Cole.

Becker, V. (1992). *The real man inside: How men can recover their identity and why women can't help*. Grand Rapids, Michigan: Zondervon Publishing House.

Bell, D. (1973). *The coming of post-industrial society: A venture in social forecasting*. New York: Basic Books.

Bell, D. H. (1981). Up from patriarchy: The male role in historical perspective. In R. A. Lewis (Ed.), *Men in difficult times: Masculinity today and tomorrow* (pp. 306-323). Englewood Cliffs, New Jersey: Prentice Hall.

Bell, D. H. (1982). *Being a man: The paradox of masculinity*. Lexington, Massachusetts: Lewis.

Bem, S. L. (1993). *The lenses of gender: Transforming the debate on sexual inequality*. New Haven, Connecticut: Yale University Press.

Beneke, T. (1993). Deep masculinity as social control: Foucault, Bly and masculinity. *Masculinities, 1*(3), 13-19.

Bergmann, B. (1986). *The economic emergence of women*. New York: Basic Books.

Bernard, J. (1981). The good-provider role: Its rise and fall. *American Psychologist, 36*, 1-12.

Biller, H. B. (1971). *Father, child, and sex role*. Lexington, Massachusetts: Lexington Books.

Blau, F. D., & Ferber, M.A. (1986). *The economics of women, men, and work*. Englewood Cliffs, New Jersey: Prentice-Hall.

Bliss, S. (1986, November-December). Beyond machismo: The new men's movement. *Yoga Journal*, pp. 36-40, 56-58.

Bliss, S. (1992). What happens at a mythopoetic men's weekend? In C. Harding (Ed.), *Wingspan: Inside the men's movement* (pp. 95-99). New York: St. Martin's Press.

Bluestone, B., & Harrison, B. (1982). *The deindustrialization of America: Plant closings, community abandonment, and the dismantling of basic industry*. New York: Basic Books.

Bly, C. (1992, March). The charismatic men's movement: Warrior wannabes, unconscious deals, and psychological booty. *Omni*, p. 6.

Bly, R. (1982, May). What men really want: A New Age interview with Robert Bly by Keith Thompson. *New Age Journal*, pp. 30-37, 50-51.

Bly, R. (1990). *Iron John: A book about men*. New York: Addison-Wesley.

Bly, R. (1992, January/February). Where are women and men today? Robert Bly and Deborah Tannen in conversation. *New Age Journal*, pp. 28-33, 92-97.

Brehm, S. (1985). *Intimate relationships*. New York: Random House.

Brenner, J., & Ramas, M. (1984). Rethinking women's oppression. *New Left Review, 144*, 33-122.

Brod, H. (1992). Work clothes and leisure suits: The class bias of the men's movement. In M. S. Kimmel & M. A. Messner (Eds.), *Men's lives* (2nd ed.) (pp. 276-287). New York: Macmillan.

Bronstein, P., & Cowan, C. P. (Eds.). (1988). *Fatherhood today: Men's changing role in the family*. New York: Wiley.

Brown, L. (1992). Essential lies: A dystopian vision of the mythopoetic men's movement. In K. L. Hagan (Ed.), *Women respond to the men's movement: A feminist collection* (pp. 93-100). San Francisco: Harper.

Burtless, G. (Ed.). (1990). *A future of lousy jobs? The changing structure of U.S. wages*. Washington, D.C.: The Brookings Institution.

Caldwell, M. & Peplau, L. (1982). Sex differences in same-sex friendship. *Sex Roles, 8*, 721-732.

Camic, C. (1987). Charisma: Its varieties, preconditions, and consequences. In J. Rabow, G. M. Platt, & M. S. Goldman (Eds.), *Advances in psychoanalytic sociology* (pp. 238-276). Malabar, Florida: Robert E. Krieger.

Cancian, F. M. (1987). *Love in America: Gender and self-development*. New York: Cambridge University Press.

Caputi, J., & MacKenzie, G. O. (1992). Pumping Iron John. In K. L. Hagan (Ed.), *Women respond to the men's movement: A feminist collection* (pp. 69-82). San Francisco: Harper.

Chafetz, J. S. (1990). *Gender equity: An integrated theory of stability and change*. Newbury Park, California: Sage.

Clatterbaugh, K. (1990). *Contemporary perspectives on masculinity: Men, women, and politics in modern society*. Boulder, Colorado: Westview Press.

Clecak, P. (1983). *America's quest for the ideal self: Dissent and fulfillment in the 60s and 70s*. New York: Oxford University Press.

Connell, R. W. (1987). *Gender and power: Society, the person and sexual politics*. Stanford, California: Stanford University Press.

Connell, R. W. (1992). Drumming up the wrong tree. *Tikkun, 7*(1), 31-36.

Coontz, S. (1992). *The way we never were: American families and the nostalgia trap*. New York: Basic Books.

Cott, N. F. (1977). *The bonds of womanhood: "Woman's sphere" in New England, 1780-1835*. New Haven, Connecticut: Yale University Press.

Cott, N. F. (1979). Passionlessness: An interpretation of Victorian sexual ideology, 1790-1850. In N. F. Cott, & E. H. Pleck (Eds.), *A heritage of her own* (pp. 107-135). New York: Simon & Schuster.

Cushman, P. (1990). Why the self is empty: Toward a historically situated psychology. *American Psychologist, 45*(5), 599-611.

Cushman, P. (1992). Psychotherapy to 1992: A historically situated interpretation. In D. K. Freedheim (Ed.), *History of psychotherapy: A century of change* (pp. 21-64). Washington, D. C.: American Psychological Association.

Dash, M. (1993). Betwixt and between in the men's movement. *Masculinities, 1*(3), 49-51.

Davidson, L., & Duberman, L. (1982). Friendship: Communication and interactional patterns in same-sex dyads. *Sex Roles, 8*, 809-822.

Davis, F. (1990). *Moving the mountain: The women's movement in America since 1960*. New York: Simon & Schuster.

Demos, J. (1982). The changing faces of fatherhood: A new exploration in American family history. In S. H. Cath, A. R. Gurwitt, & J. M. Ross (Eds.), *Father and child: Clinical and developmental perspectives* (pp. 425-450). Boston: Little, Brown.

Derlega, V., & Berg, J. (Eds.). (1987). *Self-disclosure: Theory, research, and therapy*. New York: Plenum.

Doubiago, S. (1992, April). Enemy of the mother: A feminist response to the men's movement. *Ms., 2*(5), 82-85.

Douvan, E., & Adelson, J. (1966). *The adolescent experience*. New York: Wiley.

Doyle, J. A. (1989). *The male experience* (3rd ed.), Dubuque, Iowa: William C. Brown.

Dubbert, J. L. (1979). *A man's place: Masculinity in transition*. Englewood Cliffs, New Jersey: Prentice-Hall.

Ehrenreich, B. (1983). *The hearts of men: American dreams and the flight from commitment*. Garden City, New York: Anchor Press/Doubleday.

Ehrenreich, B., & English, D. (1979). *For her own good: 150 years of the experts' advice to women.* Garden City, New York: Anchor Books.

Eisler, R. (1992). What do men really want? The men's movement, partnership, and domination. In K. L. Hagan (Ed.), *Women respond to the men's movement: A feminist collection* (pp. 43-54). San Francisco: Harper.

Ellis, K. (1994, Spring). Who's afraid of Robert Bly? Feminism, gender politics, and the mainstream media. *Masculinities, 2*(1), 8-20.

Ewen. S. (1976). *Captains of consciousness: Advertising and the social roots of the consumer culture.* New York: McGraw-Hill.

Faludi, S. (1991). *Backlash: The undeclared war against American women.* New York: Crown.

Farmer, S. (1991). *The wounded male.* New York: Ballantine Books.

Farrell, W. (1974). *The liberated man. Beyond masculinity: Freeing men and their relationships with women.* New York: Random House.

Farrell, W. (1986). *Why men are the way they are: The male-female dynamic.* New York: McGraw-Hill.

Fasteau, M. F. (1974). *The male machine.* New York: McGraw-Hill.

Fox, M., Gibbs, M., & Auerback, D. (1985). Age and gender dimensions of friendship. *Psychology of Women Quarterly, 9*, 489-501.

Franklin, C. W. (1984). *The changing definition of masculinity.* New York: Plenum Press.

Freedman, E. B., & D'Emilio, J. (1988). *Intimate matters: A history of sexuality in America.* New York: Harper & Row.

Friedan. B. (1963). *The feminine mystique.* New York: Dell.

Gabriel, T. (1990, October 14). Call of the wildmen. *New York Times Magazine*, pp. 37-47.

Gallup Opinion Index. (1975a, April). (Report No. 118). Equal Rights Amendment, pp. 20-21. Princeton, New Jersey: American Institute of Public Opinion.

Gallup Opinion Index. (1975b., July). (Report No. 121). Abortion, pp. 11-13. Princeton, New Jersey: American Institute of Public Opinion.

Gallup Poll Monthly. (1992a, January). (Report No. 316). Attitudes about abortion and impact on 1992 vote, pp. 8-9. Princeton, New Jersey: Gallup Poll.

Gallup Poll Monthly. (1992b, June). (Report No. 321). Dissatisfaction with state of nation at historic high point, pp. 16-17. Princeton, New Jersey: Gallup Poll.

Gallup Report. (1988, July). (Report No. 274). Equal Rights Amendment, p. 15. Princeton, New Jersey: Gallup Poll.

Gerson, K. (1993). *No man's land: Men's changing commitments to family and work*. New York: Basic Books.

Gilbert, R. K. (1992). Revisiting the psychology of men: Robert Bly and the mytho-poetic movement. *Journal of Humanistic Psychology, 32*(2), 41-67.

Goldberg, H. (1979). *The new male: From self-destruction to self-care*. New York: William Morrow.

Goldfield, M. (1987). *The decline of organized labor in the United States*. Chicago: University of Chicago Press.

Goode, W. J. (1992). Why men resist. In B. Thorne & M. Yalom (Eds.), *Rethinking the family: Some feminist questions* (pp. 287-310). Boston: Northeastern University Press.

Gordon, B. (1990). Men and their fathers. In R. L. Meth & R. S. Pasick (Eds.), *Men in therapy: The challenge of change* (pp. 234-246). New York: Guilford Press.

Gordon, C. (1991, November 18). What is it that men really want? *Maclean's*, p. 13.

Gordon, J. (1982). *The myth of the monstrous male—and other feminist fables*. New York: Playboy Press.

Griswold, R. L. (1993). *Fatherhood in America: A history*. New York: Basic Books.

Gross, M. L. (1978). *The psychological society: A critical analysis of psychiatry, psychotherapy, psychoanalysis, and the psychological revolution*. New York: Random House.

Hacker, H. M. (1957). The new burdens of masculinity. *Marriage and Family Living, 19*, 227-233.

Hacker, H. M. (1981). Blabbermouths and clams: Sex differences in self-disclosure in same-sex and cross-sex friendship dyads. *Psychology of Women Quarterly*, *5*, 385-401.

Hantover, J. P. (1981). The social construction of masculine anxiety. In R. A. Lewis (Ed.), *Men in difficult times: Masculinity today and tomorrow* (pp. 87-98). Englewood Cliffs, New Jersey: Prentice-Hall.

Harding, C. (1992a). What's all this about a men's movement? In C. Harding (Ed.), *Wingspan: Inside the men's movement* (pp. xi-xxii). New York: St. Martin's Press.

Harding, C. (1992b). Support groups, councils, and retreats. In C. Harding (Ed.), *Wingspan: Inside the men's movement* (pp. 76-79). New York: St. Martin's Press.

Harding, C. (1992c). Sacred ceremony or "goofy circus"? In C. Harding (Ed.), *Wingspan: Inside the men's movement* (pp. 200-201). New York: St. Martin's Press.

Harding, C. (1992d). Friendly fire. In C. Harding (Ed.), *Wingspan: Inside the men's movement* (pp. 230-231). New York: St. Martin's Press.

Harris, L. (1979). *The* Playboy *report on American men: A study of values, attitudes and goals of U.S. males 18-49 years old*. Chicago: Playboy Enterprises.

Hood, J. C. (1986). The provider role: Its meaning and measurement. *Journal of Marriage and the Family*, *48*, 349-359.

Hooks, B. (1992). Men in feminist struggle—the necessary movement. In K. L. Hagan (Ed.), *Women respond to the men's movement: A feminist collection* (pp. 111-118). San Francisco: Harper.

Johnston, J. (1992, February 23). Why *Iron John* is no gift to women. *The New York Times Book Review*, pp. 1, 28-31, 33.

Jump, T., & Haas, L. (1987). Dual-career fathers participating in child care. In M. Kimmel (Ed.), *Changing men: New directions in research on men and masculinity* (pp. 98-114). Newbury Park, California: Sage.

Kammer, J. (1992). "Male" is not a four-letter word. In C. Harding (Ed.), *Wingspan: Inside the men's movement* (pp. 63-71). New York: St. Martin's Press.

Kaufmann, Y. (1984). Analytical psychotherapy. In R. J. Corsini (Ed.), *Current psychotherapies* (3rd ed.) (pp. 108-141). Itasca, Illinois: F. E. Peacock.

Kauth, B. (1992a). *A circle of men: The original manual for men's support groups*. New York: St. Martin's Press.

Kauth, B. (1992b). Ritual in men's groups. In C. Harding (Ed.), *Wingspan: Inside the men's movement* (pp. 202-205). New York: St. Martin's Press.

Keen, S. (1991). *Fire in the belly: On being a man.* New York: Bantam Books.

Kessler, R., & McRae, J. (1982). The effects of wives' employment on the mental health of married men and women. *American Sociological Review, 47,* 216-227.

Kimmel, M. S. (1987). The contemporary "crisis" of masculinity in historical perspective. In H. Brod (Ed.), *The making of masculinities: The new men's studies* (pp. 121-153). Boston: Allen & Unwin.

Kimmel, M. S. (1989). Introduction. In M. S. Kimmel & M. A. Messner (Eds.), *Men's lives* (pp. 1-11). New York: Macmillan.

Kimmel, M. S. (1993). Pro-feminist men respond to the men's movement. *Masculinities, 1*(3), i.

Kimmel, M. S. (1995). Misogynists, masculinist mentors, and male supporters: Men's responses to feminism. In J. Freeman (Ed.), *Women: A feminist perspective* (5th ed.) (pp. 561-572). Mountain View, California: Mayfied.

Kimmel, M. S. (1996). Afterword. In M. S. Kimmel (Ed.), *The politics of manhood: Profeminist men respond to the mythopoetic men's movement (and the mythopoetic leaders answer)* (pp. 1-11). Philadelphia: Temple University Press.

Kimmel, M. S., & Kaufman, M. (1994). Weekend warriors: The new men's movement. In H. Brod & M. Kaufman (Eds.), *Theorizing masculinities* (pp. 259-288). Thousand Oaks, California: Sage.

Kinsey, A. C. (1953). *Sexual behavior in the human female.* Philadelphia: Temple University Press.

Kipnis, A. R. (1991). *Knights without armor: A practical guide for men in quest of masculine soul.* Los Angeles: Jeremy P. Tarcher.

Kipnis, A. R., & Hingston, E. (1993, January/February). Ending the war between the sexes. *Utne Reader,* pp. 69-76.

Klein, E. (1984). *Gender politics: From consciousness to mass politics.* Cambridge, Massachusetts: Harvard University Press.

Koedt, A., Levin, E., & Rapone, A. (Eds.). (1973). *Radical feminism.* New York: Quadrangle Books.

Komarovsky, M. (1974). Patterns of self-disclosure of male undergraduates. *Journal of Marriage and the Family, 36,* 677-686.

Kupers, T. (1993). Soft males and mama's boys: A critique of Robert Bly. *Masculinities, 1*(3), 55-59.

Kuznik, F. (1994, February). Death of a warrior. *Chicago,* pp. 67-69, 99-103.

Lamb, M. E. (1986). The changing roles of fathers. In M. E. Lamb (Ed.), *The father's role: Applied perspectives* (pp. 3-28). New York: John Wiley & Sons.

Lasch, C. (1977). *Haven in a heartless world: The family besieged.* New York: Basic Books.

Lasch, C. (1979). *The culture of narcissism: American life in an age of diminishing expectations.* New York: Warner Books.

Lee, J. (1991). *At my father's wedding: Reclaiming our true masculinity.* New York: Bantam Books.

Lewis, J. R. (1992). Approaches to the study of the New Age movement. In J. R. Lewis & J. G. Melton (Eds.), *Perspectives on the New Age* (pp. 1-12). Albany, New York: State University of New York Press.

Lewis, R. A. (Ed.). (1981). *Men in difficult times: Masculinity today and tomorrow.* Englewood Cliffs, New Jersey: Prentice-Hall.

Lowy, T. (1992, January). What men can't get from women. *Ladies Home Journal,* pp. 78-81.

Mazur, E., & Olver, R. (1987). Intimacy and structure: Sex differences in imagery of same-sex relationships. *Sex Roles, 16,* 539-558.

McCarthy, B. (Producer), & Ewing, W. (Director). (1990). *A gathering of men* (Video). South Burlington, Vermont: Mystic Fire Video & Public Affairs Television.

McGill, M. E. (1985). *The McGill report on male intimacy.* New York: Holt, Rinehart & Winston.

Meade, M. (1993). *Men and the water of life: Initiation and the tempering of men.* San Francisco: Harper.

Miller, S. (1983). *Men and friendship.* Boston: Houghton Mifflin.

Mintz, S., & Kellog, S. (1988). *Domestic revolutions: A social history of American family life.* New York: Free Press.

Moore, R., & Gillette, D. (1990). *King, warrior, magician, lover: Rediscovering the archetypes of the mature masculine.* San Francisco: Harper.

Morrow, L. (1991, August 19). The child is father of the man. *Time*, pp. 52-54.

Mussen, P. H., & Rutherford, E. (1963). Parent-child relations and parental personality in relations to young children's sex-role preferences. *Child Development, 34*, 589-607.

Nardi, P. M. (1992). Seamless souls: An introduction to men's friendships. In P. M. Nardi (Ed.), *Men's friendships* (pp. 1-14). Newbury Park, California: Sage.

Newman, K. S. (1988). *Falling from grace: The experience of downward mobility in the American middle class.* New York: Free Press.

Niemi, R. G., Mueller, J., & Smith, T. W. (1989). *Trends in public opinion: A compendium of survey data.* New York: Greenwood Press.

O'Neill, J. M. (1982). Gender-role conflict and strain in men's lives: Implications for psychiatrists, psychologists, and other human-service providers. In K. Solomon & N. B. Levy (Eds.), *Men in transition: Theory and therapy* (pp. 5-44). New York: Plenum Press.

Osherson, S. (1986). *Finding our fathers: The unfinished business of manhood.* New York: Free Press.

Osherson, S. (1992). *Wrestling with love: How men struggle with intimacy with women, children, parents, and each other.* New York: Lawcett Columbia.

Pasick, R. S. (1990). Raised to work. In R. L. Meth & R. S. Pasick (Eds.), *Men in therapy: The challenge of change* (pp. 35-53). New York: Guilford Press.

Pasick, R. S., Gordon, S., & Meth, R. L. (1990). Helping men understand themselves. In R. L. Meth & R. S. Pasick (Eds), *Men in therapy: The challenge of change* (pp. 152-180). New York: Guilford Press.

Piven, F. F., & Cloward, R. A. (1977). *Poor people's movements: Why they succeed, how they fail.* New York: Random House.

Pleck, J. H. (1975). Man to man: Is brotherhood possible? In N. G. Malbin (Ed.), *Old family/new family: Interpersonal relationships* (pp. 229-244). New York: Van Nostrand Reinhold.

Pleck, J. H. (1976). The male sex role: Definitions, problems, and sources of change. *Journal of Social Issues, 32*(3), 155-164.

Pleck, J. H. (1981). *The myth of masculinity*. Cambridge, Massachusetts: MIT Press.

Pleck, J. H. (1985). *Working wives/working husbands*. Beverly Hills, California: Sage.

Pleck, J. H. (1987). The contemporary man. In M. Scher, M. Stevens, G. Good, & G. A. Eichenfield (Eds.), *Handbook of counseling and psychotherapy for men* (pp. 16-38). Newbury Park, California: Sage.

Radin, N. (1982). Primary caregiving and role-sharing fathers. In M. E. Lamb (Ed.), *Nontraditional families: Parenting and child development* (pp. 173-204). Hillsdale, New Jersey: Erlbaum.

Raphael, R. (1988). *The men from the boys: Rites of passage in male America*. Lincoln, Nebraska: University of Nebraska Press.

Reisman, D. (1950). *The lonely crowd: A study of the changing American character*. New Haven, Connecticut: Yale University Press.

Reiss, I. L. (1980). *Family systems in America* (3rd ed.). New York: Holt, Rinehart & Winston.

Reiss, I. L. (1990). *An end to shame: Shaping our next sexual revolution*. Buffalo, New York: Prometheus Books.

Rieff, P. (1959). *Freud: The Mind of the Moralist*. Chicago: University of Chicago Press.

Roediger, D. R., & Foner, P. S. (1989). *Our own time: A history of American labor and the working day*. Westport, Connecticut: Greenwood Press.

Rosen, R. (1992, Fall). Stand by your woman. *Dissent*, 539-541.

Rotenberg, K. (1986). Same-sex patterns and sex differences in the trust-value basis of children's friendship. *Sex Roles, 15*, 613-626.

Rotundo, E. A. (1987). Patriarchs and participants: A historical perspective on fatherhood in the United States. In M. Kaufman (Ed.), *Essays by men on pleasure, power and change* (pp. 64-80). Toronto: Oxford University Press.

Rotundo, E. A. (1993). *American manhood: Transformations in masculinity from the revolution to the modern era*. New York: Basic Books.

Ryan, M. P. (1975). *Womanhood in America: From colonial times to the present*. New York: New Viewpoints.

Samuels, A. (1992, Spring). Men under scrutiny. *Psychological Perspectives*, pp. 26-61.

Schwalbe, M. (1993). Why mythopoetic men don't flock to NOMAS. *Masculinities*, *1*(3), 68-72.

Schwalbe, M. (1996). *Unlocking the iron cage: The men's movement, gender politics, and American culture*. New York: Oxford University Press.

Sears, R. R., Maccoby, E. E., & Levin, H. (1957). *Patterns of child rearing*. Evanston, Illinois: Peterson.

Seidman, S. (1992). *Embattled eros: Sexual politics and ethics in contemporary America*. New York: Routledge.

Sherrod, D. (1987). The bonds of men: Problems and possibilities of close male relationships. In H. Brod (Ed.), *The making of masculinities: The new men's studies* (pp. 213-239). Boston: Allen & Unwin.

Shewey, D. (1992, February 11). Town meeting in the hearts of men. *The Village Voice*, *37*(6), pp. 36-46.

Simkin, J. S., & Yontef, G. M. (1984). Gestalt therapy. In R. J. Corsini (Ed.), *Current psychotherapies* (3rd ed.) (pp. 279-319). Itasca, Illinois: F. E. Peacock.

Skjej, E., & Rabkin, R. (1981). *The male ordeal: Role crisis in a changing world*. New York: G. P. Putnam's Sons.

Staines, G., Pottick, K. J., & Fudge, D. A. (1986). Wives' employment and husbands' attitudes toward work and life. *Journal of Applied Psychology*, *71*, 118-128.

Stanton, D. (1991, October). Inward, Ho! *Esquire*, pp. 113-128.

Starker, S. (1989). *Oracle at the supermarket: The American preoccupation with self-help books*. New Brunswick, New Jersey: Transaction Books.

Stearns, P. N. (1979). *Be a man! Males in modern society*. New York: Holmes & Meier.

Stearns, P. N. (1990). *Be a man! Males in modern society* (2nd ed.). New York: Holmes & Meier.

Steinem, G. (1992). Forward. In K. L. Hagan (Ed.), *Women respond to the men's movement: A feminist collection* (pp. v-ix). San Francisco: Harper.

Stephens, J. D. (1986). *The transition from capitalism to socialism*. Urbana, Illinois: University of Illinois Press.

Stoltenberg, J. (1995, Spring). Male virgins, blood covenants & family values. *On the Issues: The Progressive Woman's Quarterly*, pp. 25-29, 51-52.

Thomas, D. (1993). *Not guilty: The case in defense of men*. New York: William Morrow.

Thompson, R. A. (1983). The father's case in child custody disputes: The contributions of psychological research. In M. E. Lamb & A. Sagi (Eds.), *Fatherhood and family policy* (pp. 53-100). Hillsdale, New Jersey: Lawrence Erlbaum Associates.

Tschann, J. (1988). Self-disclosure in adult friendship: Gender and marital status differences. *Journal of Social and Personal Relationships, 5*, 65-81.

Van Horn, S. H. (1988). *Women, work, and fertility, 1900-1986*. New York: New York University Press.

Vanden Bos, G. K., Cummings, N. A., & DeLeon, P. H. (1992). A century of psychotherapy: Economic and environmental influences. In D. K. Freedheim (Ed.), *History of psychotherapy: A century of change* (pp. 65-102). Washington, D.C.: American Psychological Association.

Veroff, J., Douvan, E., & Kulka, R. A. (1981). *The inner American: A self-portrait from 1957 to 1976*. New York: Basic Books.

Wachtel, P. L. (1983). *The poverty of affluence: A psychological portrait of the American way of life*. New York: Free Press.

Wagenheim, J. (1990, September/October). The secret life of men. *New Age Journal*, pp. 40-45, 106-113.

Weinstein, F., & Platt, G. M. (1969). *The wish to be free: Society, psyche and value change*. Berkeley: University of California Press.

Weinstein, F., & Platt, G. M. (1973). *Psychoanalytic sociology: An essay on the interpretation of historical data and the phenomena of collective behavior*. Baltimore: John Hopkins University Press.

Welter, B. (1966). The cult of true motherhood: 1820-1860. *American Quarterly, 18*, 151-174.

Whyte, W. H. (1956). *The organization man*. New York: Simon & Schuster.

Williams, D. (1985). Gender, masculinity-femininity, and emotional intimacy in same-sex friendship. *Sex Roles, 12*, 587-600.

Wirth, L. (1938/1957). Urbanism as a way of life. In P. K. Hatt & A. J. Reiss, Jr. (Eds.), *Cities and society: The revised reader in urban sociology* (pp. 46-63). New York: Free Press.

Yankelovich, D. (1981). *New rules: Searching for self-fulfillment in a world turned upside down.* New York: Random House.

Zaretsky, E. (1976). *Capitalism, the family, and personal life.* New York: Harper & Row.

i want morebooks!

Buy your books fast and straightforward online - at one of world's fastest growing online book stores! Free-of-charge shipping and environmentally sound due to Print-on-Demand technologies.

Buy your books online at
www.get-morebooks.com

Kaufen Sie Ihre Bücher schnell und unkompliziert online – auf einer der am schnellsten wachsenden Buchhandelsplattformen weltweit! Versandkostenfrei und dank Print-On-Demand umwelt- und ressourcenschonend produziert.

Bücher schneller online kaufen
www.morebooks.de

VDM Verlagsservicegesellschaft mbH
Dudweiler Landstr. 99
D - 66123 Saarbrücken

Telefon: +49 681 3720 174
Telefax: +49 681 3720 1749

info@vdm-vsg.de
www.vdm-vsg.de

Made in the USA
Coppell, TX
18 November 2022